2

TextAppeal – For Guys!

The Ultimate Texting Guide

Michael Masters

Published by Michael Masters

Createspace Version

Copyright © 2012 Michael Masters

ISBN-13: 978-1469983837

ISBN-10: 1469983834

Table of Contents

Part I - Intro to Texting

I am better than you at texting.

Why am I so good? Two reasons: I started texting in Asia about five years before it even arrived in the US and I understand the dynamics of relationships like a chef understands alcoholism. Want to get good? Read on.

The Old Lady

I am sitting in the Sears automotive waiting room. There is an older woman sitting across from me. She doesn't look very happy sitting with her hands in her lap, forced to focus on the silence. I have my laptop open, tethered with the Internet on my jail-broken iPhone. I am busy IM'ing someone on Skype while texting someone on my phone.

While I am geeking out in the corner she gets up the guts to say something. "Are you texting?" she asked. "Yep, got a few conversations going here" I said, motioning at my computer. She says, "I don't really understand that kinda thing very much, I feel like it is so impersonal, I mean, why don't young people talk face to face anymore, all they do is text all the time."

I didn't want to openly disagree with her but she was clearly bashing something she didn't understand. Texting has allowed us to connect more not less. We are able to fire off a text to ten people at the same time. Drop a note to a friend when calling might not be appropriate. A text can be a permanent record of something useful like an address or a phone number. You can text someone when a phone call can be intimidating and you can text multiple people when phone calls would take too much time.

Texting is very useful and is here to stay but it has a lot of limitations. It is very difficult to pick up tone in a text. You may want a response back quickly but you may not get one. Texting can be annoying, easily ignored, or cause feelings to get hurt. If you are not careful with what you say, texts can be a permanent record of what you may not want others to know.

Even with all of these disadvantages, texting is incredibly useful and will only increase in functionality in the next few years. Unfortunately, no matter how much it improves, there still will be a lot of communication problems associated with texting.

However, I can teach you how to get really excellent results, and very often these results are even better than talking to someone in person. I can teach you how to avoid the typical pitfalls of texting and the BIG NO NOs that will get you ignored and erased. With some simple strategy, you will be able to get her to text you back immediately with the answer you want to hear! Does saying the right thing really make that much a difference?? Absofrickenlutly it does!

On many, many occasions I have taken a guy or girl's phone and within minutes totally changed the results people were getting. (One time I was texting an NBA ball player from my friend's phone, he had no clue…) The point is this… It is very easy for you to control a conversation over text with a few rules and strategies. Don't underestimate what is possible in this simple medium.

"If you discipline yourself to take that extra 30 seconds to send something smarter than what you normally would, you will get extraordinary results"

Normal Conversation vs. Texting

Texting is very similar to normal conversation but with one HUGE difference; you have time to think of a good answer. Remember the last time you got into a verbal fight with someone and only afterwards did you think of something really good to say?? You know what I mean, you ruminated for hours/days on how to respond.

"Mike you are such an arrogant ass." I respond weakly, "Well you… are…" my eyes flick around looking for something witty but the room is as empty as my head. Later I come up with a deluge of excellent responses, which I write down in an angry email that I will never send. God… I hate my sister!

This is the killer advantage to texting that few people take advantage of. They don't realize that they can craft a very witty, cool response to whatever anyone says to them. If you discipline yourself to take that extra 30 seconds to send something much smarter than what you normally would, you will get extraordinary results.

Not only that, but you can step out of the emotional moment, in other words, you have time to calm down so that you can say the right thing later. What a killer opportunity if you tend to say the wrong thing to women.

"You should never hang on for the person's next text, ready to fire off a response. This communicates need, the biggest dating buzz kill"

Thinking of a Great Answer

Don't underestimate the extra time you have to analyze a situation. I am pretty good at it so I can fire off a response pretty fast, however, I will often create a response and then sit on it for a good five to ten minutes, or however long it took them to get back to me. Point is, take your time and create a response that creates more attraction and pushes your wit muscles.

You may not feel that you are the most attractive guy, but little do you know that this really isn't all that important. How many times have you seen a really hot girl with an average guy and you've said, "WTF? Why is she with HIM??" The answer is very simple, he is smart, and knows how to entertain/challenge her. Women date men far more often for what they say, and who they are, than how they look. Don't underestimate this, if you say the right things, super hot girls will be attracted to you like flies to... well, shit.

With that said, I have known some really bright good-looking guys that would repel women, more than a meth-head case of halitosis. Why? Because they were socially awkward, not taking the time to learn what makes a women uncomfortable, and/or not having a clue how to entertain/challenge. Attracting women takes some serious observation of the opposite sex, and their reactions. Hopefully, I can help you figure this out a LOT faster and get you results instantly.

Intelligence is one the most attractive qualities for a woman (Power, is probably number one, but intelligence is a form of power). Sexual selection based on intelligence is actually a theory of Charles Darwin only recently mathematically possible to prove. So! Flex that grey matter!!

I talk about this a little bit more on my website

http://tinyurl.com/3oyme4h

Legacy of IM

IM (instant messaging) is pretty much like live conversation. You have a little bit more time to think about your response but since you know that your audience is on the other line waiting, you must stay on the computer rapt for their response. I think this is why people multitask with IM; either talking to 10 others at the same time or surfing the net.

Personally, I hate IM because it is such a time waster. I use it more like texting and only get back to people when I want to. Most people used IM before they ever learned to text and **try to use it similarly**. This is a mistake in the realm of texting. You should never hang on the person's next words, ready to fire off a response. This communicates need, the biggest dating buzz kill. I am not telling you to not respond, only to be aware that it is far more preferable to make the girl wait five minutes, an hour, or a day.

Please remember this translates to Facebook too. DO NOT be instant messaging with your target, it is just a bad idea until you build some real attraction first. Too many things can go wrong with IM at the beginning of your first interactions.

Part II - Why Texting Rocks

Responding by not Responding

Texting can be a huge time saver. If every text equaled a phone call, I can't imagine that you would have time in the day to make or take all the calls. Texting allows you to get back to the texter when it is convenient or maybe not get back to them at all.

Very often you may not want to respond. Often this sends a stronger message than responding. That person asking you to cover their shift at work or maybe a girl that was a bit bitchy, you may not want to respond to. Not responding makes people create assumptions; this is a very effective communicator since we all are our own worst critics. I will expand on this a little later.

"A lot of people don't understand the Slow Mo component to texting, they send a text back immediately expecting an immediate response. This is a texting no no..."

Forcing you to be Clear

This defines Twitter. You have to put your thoughts in a very clear, succinct way. This is a good thing! It forces you to focus and not ramble in a phone conversation trying to figure out how to ask her out on a date. This is another thing that makes texting so great, it allows you to ask her out without feeling nearly the same level of anxiety a phone conversation might produce.

Texting is Killer Practice

When you are bantering over text you have the time to think about things and put your wittiest foot forward. This translates very well into real life and can be killer practice if you suck at this. In a text you can push the limits of what you might be comfortable saying and then carry that into normal conversation. Texting simply helps you take your game to a higher level.

Text is just a Conversation in Slow-Mo

Texting is the same as a normal conversation, but because of a time lag, a lot of people break rules they would never break in real life. If she does not text you back right away is it okay to send another text? Ask yourself this question: Would it be okay in a normal conversation to keep asking the same question without a response??

A lot of people don't understand the Slow Mo component of texting and they text back immediately expecting an immediate response. This is a huge texting no no... a very good reason for you to put your phone away after a text and go do something else. Dwelling on why she has not texted you back yet will only drive you mad.

Easier to set a date

While I think it is a great thing to get someone on the phone, initially it may not be the right thing to do. Texting leaves a level of mystery that can be punctured by a phone convo. This mystery allows her to fill in the gaps of her knowledge with (usually) positive assumptions about you. Now, if you say the right things and show her a good time it is quite easy to ask her out. All you have to do is wait until she is laughing, and responding well, then ask her to meet you at a very non-threatening place, like a coffee shop.

Part III - How texting can be a huge problem

Texting can have a lot of problems that you must be aware of so you don't make all the mistakes that I have made! The most crippling being...

The Wrong Text to the Wrong Person

Me: Hey, are you sore too? My pubic bone is all bruised!!

Ten minutes later my co-worker texts me back, "I think you got the wrong Sarah! lol" I get to work only to find my text written on one of the white boards in the office. Oops...

This of course is the worst when you are dating multiple people and get your wires crossed. I can't tell you how many times I have gotten text conversations confused or asked out the wrong girl via text. You can imagine my surprise when the face didn't match up with the person I thought I was texting. Nice Mike...

Permanent Record!

My friend Kyle was a complete idiot. Not only was he lying to everyone around him but he was stupid enough to do it in writing. When we eventually all got together and compared notes, we had text records dates and times on our phones. Kyle not only got proven wrong but he could have been tried and convicted with the undeniable evidence we had. So am I saying that if you are a cheater you should be careful what you text? Yes! But hopefully you are not and you understand the message. What you say can be pulled up months later and it is wise to watch your tongue...

Limited

The lady at Sears did have a bit of a point. There is a limitation to texting since it is not very face-to-face. It is like the gamer that believes he has a social life because he has "online friends."

Just because you are texting does not mean you have a relationship with someone. This is only the flirting/foreplay stage. It is the time to see if you are well matched. Until you have physical contact, anything can happen, but texting can set the stage for anything to happen! Texting can be that powerful.

"It is pretty cool to be able to send the text "I can't stand her!" with a vomiting smiley face."

The Problem with Communicating Tone

In America, I find communicating tone to be an issue but this was not a problem when I lived in Japan. Sorry to say it, but Asia has our butts kicked in texting. Text there is just modified email, you can send as many as you want, it has no size limit, there is no charge, and you can send pictures/video no problem. Text has been that way since 2000. The coolest thing about text in Asia is the addition of emoticons and simple gif files. It is pretty cool to send the text "I can't stand her!" with a vomiting smiley face. Not only is this stuff funny, and communicates tone better than any words. In the States we have a few of these tone softeners, but it is so much easier to get caught in a misunderstanding.

I am sure you have sent something like this before and gotten bit.

"God, you are such a bitch!"

You got your ass chewed because tone was impossible to convey.

But if you sent… "God, you are such a bitch! =)"

Very, very different feel right!?

Don't be afraid to use things like LOL or happy faces to soften and clarify your meanings. It honestly is shocking how such a small thing can save a potentially bad situation from getting out of control. I want you to be challenging to the girl you text but we also want them to know we are being playful.

IYHS

IN YOUR HEAD SYNDROME (IYHS) a friend of mine came up with this term and I think it is awfully true. Basically what this means is that you are creating a fantasy in your head that this particular girl is the most amazing desirable woman, that you have ever met online, in a chat room, on Worlds of Warcraft. (Come on, you and I both know that she is 300 pounds with 5 suckling babes)

This is a huge problem in the age of the Internet because we are connecting less and less face-to-face and are not able to really know the person we are talking to. Texting only adds to this, the communication is incredibly short and the assumptions we make from it are often ten times beyond reality. However this can also work for you since, like I said before, there is a component of mystery that you can convey. I only want you to be on the other side of that mystery, not the one enamored with a fantasy that will only disappoint you later.

Remember texting is **your** tool to build attraction with her. Do not allow it to carry you away into assumptions far beyond reality.

Men and women communicate differently

In a lot of ways men and women are the same but in a few critical areas we are vastly different. One of the largest differences is that women are much better communicators than men. In other words, women like to talk. This is why there are so many women writers, journalists, talk show hosts, etc.

This often works to your advantage since she will probably be more chatty than you. This is a good opportunity to either tease her about it, or not communicate as much, driving her crazy. Women are usually very frustrated that men don't communicate to the same degree, but this is a good thing since it will increase her interest in you. In other words it isn't necessary for you to ramble as much as she does, and by not doing so, you increase attraction.

Part IV - A quick guide to the massive topic of creating and maintaining attraction

"Attraction boils down to one thing: Sexual tension. And maintaining that tension boils down to one thing: Power balance."

Okay, I am going to get a little heavy on you here! I can give you a ton of tips, tricks, rules and no nos but they are relatively worthless if you don't understand the purpose and meaning behind what you should and shouldn't do. So pay close attention to this chapter and as you walk through the later chapters try to paste those tips to this framework. If you get this, you will be able to write your own rules, strategies and no nos!

Attraction is a pretty massive topic and one I can't completely cover in a few pages but I will do my best!

Attraction boils down to one thing: Sexual tension. And maintaining that tension boils down to one thing: Power balance.

Sexual Tension

All attraction can be boiled down to one simple concept, tension. Humans and animals are programmed to seek out the highest quality mate that they can, in order to have the highest quality offspring. How do they gauge this? Tension.

Humans and animals constantly push the boundaries of what is acceptable, to test that tension in a potential mate. This is why one must accept and escalate the tension being created by the other person as well as create your own.

Quick example: Last week I was out with a group of people in Japan and a girl that I found very attractive. While ordering a beer I realize that I left my iPhone at the last bar, "AHH! Crap!" I bail out of the bar and go in a full sprint over half a mile. Then, I sprint back with my iPhone in tow. The humidity is literally 90% and I am wearing jeans and a cotton tee, so you can only imagine how much sweat is running down my face and soaking my shirt.

"Whew! Found it!" I said as the girl I like shrinks away from me in

12

disgust. "Oh my god, you sweating so much!" she says in a thick Indonesian accent. I smile at her and move to hug her, she recoils again this time curling her lip. "Don't touch me! You gross!" She takes a towel out of her bag and throws it down in front of me, "You wipe your face." I look at her with a smile, "No, do it for me," I lean my head her direction and buckle my knees a bit to accommodate her tiny stature. "No! I no want to touch!" she says even though she is now holding the towel and is reaching halfway towards me. The scenario repeats itself three more times and my male friend watches, horribly amused. Finally she touches the towel to my face and starts to wipe off my dripping sweat. I stop her, grin broadly, take the towel away and walk to the bathroom to rinse off.

To the normal observer this interaction would seem a little strange, maybe even rude on my part but I understand this well and I will play it to my advantage every time. This was the first time I met the girl above and it is exactly the time when boundaries are pushed and tension is created. She was a bit of a princess and being busty and gorgeous she was used to getting her way with all men.

There was no way I was going to be one of her minions of worshipful men, waiting in the wings for an inkling of a chance. Screw that, I **am** going to take the risk to piss her off. I am going to take the risk of being totally myself. I am NOT going to comply to her every need. When she finally came around and bent to my will, not only did I shatter her bitch shield, I responded flawlessly to her challenge, creating oodles of tension and making myself ridiculously interesting to her.

This is a bit of an extreme example and would be a bit hard to emulate if you didn't feel really, really comfortable in your own shoes. This story shows a lot of tension being created very quickly by riding the fine line of what is socially acceptable.

Let me give you another example to make this even clearer. I have a client of mine that is 38, good looking, wealthy, and quite a famous body builder. You would think that this guy would have no problem picking up and keeping the ladies. But, clearly he wouldn't be hiring me if this were the case. Let me tell you his story and you can see how he destroys tension every chance he gets.

Bruce met Jessica at a body building expo in Las Vegas and they instantly connected. The next three days they were inseparable, baring their souls to each other. Bruce instantly assumed that he had found his soul mate and he fell head first in love. Jessica seemed quite smitten too but she wasn't looking to settle down quite yet, and the idea of a long distance relationship didn't please her.

For the next six months Bruce pursued Jessica, pushing to have a relationship even though they still hadn't had sex. Things got worse when Bruce was selected to be on the cover of a famous bodybuilding magazine. Bruce then pulled in favors to get her on the cover with him. Jessica was not a competitive body builder, only a fitness model and it was relatively unheard of for someone like this to be on the magazine cover. Jessica, excited to move her career forward, jumped at the opportunity, as well as accepting Bruce's offer to pay for her flight, hotel, and rental car.

Over six more times, Bruce paid for Jessica to meet him at body building events. At this point Jessica was cooling, and Bruce was getting upset. Half the time she would cancel at the last minute, and the other half she would find ways to not spend time with him.

When Bruce looked at her facebook one day he really lost it, there in her tagged photos, was her with the same guy over and over, and in one shot they were kissing. Bruce was crushed, furious, and became obsessed with getting her attentions back. But it won't happen, he crushed any tension that was ever created and his situation is unfixable.

What did Bruce do to kill the tension?

- He came on too strong setting off her fear response

- He smothered her with attention, and she couldn't breathe

- He ignored the fact that she wasn't reciprocating his attraction

- He wasn't receptive to the tons of "hints" showing her lack of interest

- He was too polite and never initiated sex, which made him look weak

- He made relationship demands before she was even remotely ready

- He acted jealous and tried to demand sexual exclusivity

- He kept paying for her and allowed her to use him

Everything that Bruce did was poisoning the tension. The nice generous guy move, pushed her into taking advantage, and how can anyone respect someone they are taking advantage of. Then, he set off her fear response by demanding a relationship when they hadn't even bumped uglies. He couldn't have done a better job to make her slam the attraction door.

Ironically, her actions did everything to build tension with Bruce! She was distant, unavailable, seeing other men, a bitch, and not reciprocating any of his gifts. This drove Bruce mad and he fell into obsession with a girl really not worth his energy. I have spent the last two weeks working with Bruce to let this girl go, but he has created such a massive fantasy around her that it might be easier to convince him to move to Thailand and become a ladyboy.

Building tension is not only about what to do, but what NOT to do.

Tension is positive!

Please understand that tension does not have to be negative like in the above example. It actually can be very positive! Tension is only expression of power perceived by the opposite sex as attractive. Here are some more examples of what tension can be:

Beauty

Intelligence

Confidence

Fearlessness

Kindness

Fitness

Sexuality

Creativity

15

Why is the musician on stage so bloody fascinating to the people watching? Because there is a tension, granted it is only one way, but we adore that person who has something we don't have. We adore that person that other people adore! This is why movie stars marry movie stars, they simply can't find that tension elsewhere or be able to maintain power balance. Beyonce will never date you, because there could never be tension or balance.

Just like the musician or the actor, when you excel at something and you are proud and unapologetic of who you are, tension is created for the person that may not excel to the same degree in that area. When one finds another that has equal power in different areas and mutual respect for the others' qualities exist, you have a level of tension that can lead to a long, very exciting relationship.

However, it is your job to make sure that your power is well expressed, that you are proud of it, and that you don't apologize for it. It is also your job to defend your boundaries, your sense of right and wrong without anger or self-doubt. It is your job to be comfortable in your own skin and radiate a level of confidence great enough to attract that woman that you think is out of your league.

Here is a little more info on sexual tension in a video by Divorce Guru Kim Hess and myself. This video was originally aimed at women but guys can still get a lot out of it. http://vimeo.com/12219750

My website also has some more info on it http://tinyurl.com/3cknyqx make sure you follow the links at the bottom to read everything on the subject.

Maintaining sexual tension with Power Balance

Every relationship demands balance because without it tension no longer exists and without tension there is boredom. This is ultimately the reason for the failure of most relationships, including friendships. When I explain this concept to most people they baulk because they seem to think that tension is a negative quality, but nothing could be further from the truth. The reason we need tension is because we need to grow. We become better people when we are with someone that pushes our worldview or just balances out our poor behavior.

I have an excellent friend in Southern California. He is a very, very intelligent guy that looks like a member of the Hells Angels. Jon affectionately calls me a scrawny, noodle-armed tree-hugger. (In my defense I am 6 foot and 190 pounds) Why are we friends? Because we push each other's boundaries in a way that is respectful and encourages mutual growth. If at one point I have learned all I can from Jon or one of us damages the balance, the friendship will end. This is identical to a relationship with the opposite sex and unless it is maintained and nurtured, it will fail.

The Teeter-Totter

Imagine you are standing on a teeter-totter with your target. Now picture yourself taking a large step towards her, if she doesn't move what will happen? Her side will head toward the ground, and once on the ground she will think it is rather boring there and decide to step off. What will happen to you? Well, you will go crashing to the ground hard enough to shatter your teeth.

This is what happens when you move aggressively towards or away from your target, you destroy the balance and both of you end up on the ground.

There are tons of ways to maintain and nurture power balance but the truth is that you probably already do most of them with your friends and family. All you need to do is learn to apply them a little bit more toward the opposite sex and realize that the maintenance of balance in a physical relationship is ten times more important than you once thought

"How many relationships older than 5 years do you know that are still successful? 1 or 2? None? Does this tell you something?"

Sexual Tension examples

Often the less moral Pick Up Artist is able to pick up because he creates a negative tension with a woman. He often creates attraction by aggressively making fun of her in a way she cannot easily defend. This ego rape is a negative tension and one that can't be maintained. He will inevitably become bored of her and move on to his next target in order to support his sex/new woman habit. Not a positive cycle but it illustrates the negative addictive side of sexual tension.

How about the woman that follows *The Rules?* She is creating a form of unsustainable tension by forcing the man to wait and pursue. What happens when he finally lands his prey? The sexual tension is often broken and things fade UNLESS in the waiting a new tension was created. Something like mutual respect and enjoyment of the other person but more often than not the only tension was sexual.

How about the really, really nice guy? He buys the girl flowers and calls her four times a day. There is no tension here and unless she is doing exactly the same thing, the relationship will fail due to boredom on her part and the guy will be all butt-hurt because, "The nice guy never wins" This is bullshit of course, the proper belief is, "The ass kisser never wins." It is perfectly okay to be a nice guy as long as you can sense the balance and back off when it is appropriate.

Now the typical girl that falls in love with every guy she meets and is constantly crushed because men are all bastards. She meets a cool guy, resists for a week or two over sex and then finally explodes with passion and screws his brains out. She now completely loses mental control and thinks she is part of the cast of Titanic. She comes on WAY too strong and takes one giant step forward on the teeter-totter and... His side goes crashing to the ground. The balance is crushed and the guy unfairly takes the rap.

Maintaining the balance

How many relationships older than 5 years do you know that are still successful? 1 or 2? None? Does this tell you something? It is extremely difficult for a long-term relationship to stay exciting or to maintain balance. I am a skeptic but at the same time I do think the only way to make a run at things is through understanding balance and learning to maintain it.

A long time ago something changed when I lost 20 pounds and started to model in LA. My girlfriend and best friend of two years suddenly didn't want to touch me. She complained that my shoulder was too boney to sleep on. She tried to get me to eat junk food and would buy my favorite beer and drink it in front of me. Not long after, she cheated on me and we separated.

What happened? The balance was shaken, I lost weight, she felt insecure about herself, and threatened by the attractive women I would meet. The relationship was sabotaged by her and permanently ruined.

This balance is something the two of you must always be alert and aware of. A relationship built on positive tension and proper power balance is going to last a hell of a long time. And don't think that you can let up on that tension and have a good relationship. That is not how the human mind works and I am convinced it is the major reason we fall out of love with our partner.

I know this is a little beyond a book on texting but this short list is absolutely applicable to getting her, keeping her, and actually enjoying it.

Conditions necessary for positive tension and healthy relationships:

- Independent strength – you are strong and you do not need the other's strength to survive.

- Intelligence – equal and balanced, both of you look up to the other.

- Opinionated – Lovers don't need to have the same world-view, in fact to push your partner to a new understanding of the world is a beautiful gift.

- Demanding of respect – Without this, no love can maintain. You must be willing to lose what you love in order to protect who you are.

- Continuous desire for growth – This must be present and equal in both partners, you don't need to be moving in the same direction but you must be moving at the same speed.

- Equal physical/sexual attraction – If you can look at your lover and say, "My god… is that who I am going to make love to tonight?" Wow, is there any greater positive sexual tension than this? (However, Love sheds pounds and fixes hairlines)

- Intellectual connection – Intelligence is not enough, you must love and enjoy the beautiful pattern of thought the other person weaves, knitting yourself into their being.

- Fun, Humor and delight – Without laughter and joy, what relationship can be whole?

- Communication – This is the glue that binds your resonance, without it your pattern will unravel and the connection will be lost. It is a skill and one you have to constantly maintain.

Wrap up

If the concepts of sexual tension and power balance are not stamped to your brain, go back and read this chapter again! Draw a little teeter totter and imagine what will happen if you text her "I really like you" before she is ready to take that step. Imagine the two of you balancing on either side and she starts to back away emotionally, do you run towards her to save the relationship? Clearly not

Now, if you really understand these concepts it becomes relatively easy use texting as a remarkable tool too affect that balance and tension.

Part V - Rules and No no's

Have you ever studied a foreign language? Inevitably they start you off with basics and rules. Do fluent people follow these rules? Not really... but they are aware of them since they all started there. Therefore, the first step in the direction of texting fluency is to understand and apply the rules. After the rules have been burned into your brain, you can get a little more flexible. However, for now you must stick to the rules. If you don't and get burned, remember, I told you so! And go back to the rules. I break the rules all the time; I can because I understand the language of texting like Einstein gets math. I understand how to get away with breaking them to get to my goal faster. Can I explain to you how to do this?? Absolutely not, I can explain how to take the first step and from there you can start kicking some texting ass, and this starts by avoiding a few of the NO NOs!

Some of these will be obvious to you but I would like to give you a good mental kick-in-the-ass reminder that they are often un-repairable deal breakers.

Drunken Texting

My friend Lacy has a problem: whenever she gets the slightest bit buzzed, the phone comes out and she starts "drunk texting" every guy that wants to sleep with her. It is so bad that we literally have to confiscate her phone or she won't talk to us.

Is drunk texting that bad? YES!!! Especially if you wouldn't have texted her when you were sober! And of course the things that come out of your mouth... Ouch! Have you ever noticed that some of your most embarrassing moments have involved alcohol and the opposite sex? Undoubtedly you are going to say the wrong thing and turn her off like hammer to a light bulb.

Don't do this! Give the phone to a friend, enjoy the people around you, and screw up with one of them instead.

Texting Shorthand

Texting shorthand is one of my pet peeves. Here are some examples from someone that has moved this horrible habit to Twitter:

"o #1 doesn't wana talk so u go2 #2??????like that?"

"I can listn2my "bad ass beats" and ull b content?"

"ugta live a lil&do it1 day,i get the hotest gossip"

What??? Are you kidding me??? I haven't edited these AT ALL... this is exactly what I pulled off her Twitter page. I can guarantee she learned this from texting on a phone without a keyboard. Yes, I know you can fit more but why?? Not only is it really, really hard to understand but it's low class. Can't fit it all? Just send a second fricken text and get a phone with a keyboard.

Emo/Important Stuff Texting

"I don't have anymore work for you this month," said the contractor. I immediately called, got no answer and received another text, "Working can't answer," he said. I text back, "What do you mean?? I thought we had 3 months of work left?" He responded with, "I hired someone more skilled with flooring and I am going with him." At this point I was pissed, "You F-ing little pussy, you fire me over text!?"

No I didn't say that... I wish... However, I did say, "You fired me over text? That was a coward move," and let it go.

TEXT IS NOT THE PLACE FOR ANYTHING SERIOUS

Texting a break up or negative news is as spineless as it is to give someone the finger from your car as they exit the off ramp. NEVER handle something over text that should be handled in person or on the phone. This just shows that you are a weakling that deserves a good slapping.

So next time you want to send her a text like:

- Where is this relationship going?

- I really want to talk about us

- Why are you such a bitch right now

- You really pissed me off last night

- Who is this guy I keep seeing on your facebook

- I think we should see other people

AHHHHH!!!!! This garbage is the emotional bomb you just lit the fuse on. Getting emotional or serious over text is going to get you ignored, avoided, and probably laughed at. Keep your feelings to yourself in the beginning, don't be needy, don't be emo, and if you **must...** handle these topics face to face. Otherwise she is going to turn to her roommate, phone in hand and say, "Oh gawd... look at this bullshit."

Texting is a frivolous place to do a little relationship fencing. (The sport, not construction of.) It simply isn't content-rich enough to convey anything too deep, without her assuming the worst. Do yourself a favor, swallow your fear, and pick up the phone.

"When you text the opposite sex, you and they are being tested, and a series of questions slowly get answered. Do they like me? Are they needy? Is he funny? Is she intelligent? Does he just want sex?"

Needy "I'm on Crack" Texting

This is hands-down the number one mistake people make with texting. The frustrating part is that "crack texting" is SOOO avoidable! I have to admit, I get the urge to do the same stupid stuff when I'm really into a girl. I will catch myself hitting the send button before I have even finished reading her text. If she doesn't text me back right away, I send another one, and another and another... I send junk texts to get her to say something. I froth at the mouth, desperate for her response! I act like that monkey at the zoo; masturbating and flinging his feces at the crowd!! Pay attention to me!!!

DON'T BE THIS PERSON

When you text the opposite sex, you and they are being tested, and a series of questions slowly get answered: Do they like me? Are they needy? Is he funny? Is she intelligent? Does he just want sex? Is she a prude? Is he/she relationship material?

This test is very easy to mess up and most often is done in the first five minutes face-to-face. Texting is different; you are able to draw out the conversation to present an excellent image. BUT you must, must, must be patient... The hotter they are, the less you should be texting them. Don't be needy!!!

Junk Texting

Junk texts are the boring texts, the empty ones and the ones that just don't need to be stated. Learning to write has taught me one very valuable lesson. Edit, edit, edit. This means that I will always remove rather than add to something. Keep it lean and interesting, not fat and dull. Those extra fillers that you send her?? Waste of her time and it makes you look stupid.

"Wow, the Lakers are playing awesome tonight!" Unless she is a sports fan, this is just a junk text trying to get her attention. Remember part of attraction is not making yourself so available.

Sexting

I would say that guys sexting girls is the number one pet peeve of women. Just because you are horny doesn't mean she is too. Maybe you think just a slightly sexual text would be okay? No, don't go here, if you haven't slept together yet this is one of the worst things you can do.

I hope you get this, women are not nearly as sexual as men, your average woman masturbates once/twice a week, how often do you masturbate? Daily? More than once a day? Does this tell you something? This certainly doesn't mean she won't want to rut like pigs in mud, but she probably doesn't have that feeling yet.

Usually, when a guy sends a slightly dirty text to a new target he elicits nothing but discomfort. She might ignore what you said, or try to come back with something, mildly sexual, but trust me she doesn't like the corner you just backed her into. Now she is uncomfortable, caught between making you happy and not being okay with you being sexual. She worries that all you want is sex, and probably don't take her seriously.

Maybe it's true, maybe all you want is sex, but does that make it okay to sext her? No, it is going to set off her fear response ruining any chance you had of getting her in to bed. Want sex? Probably the fastest way to get it, is to not pressure her for it. Making a girl feel safe, especially in the sex department is one of the most effective ways to get her clothes off.

Trust me on this one, the more you push for sex the more difficult it will be to remove her pants. Sexting is a bad idea, don't do it.

I am going to give an exception here, if you manage to make it funny and very random, you can send something sexual to test the waters. I will say something like:

Me: I remember when we first met, you were totally checking out my ass...

Her: I was not!!

or

Me: I am a little nervous to meet you tomorrow, I just want you to know I am not easy.

Her: Whatever, you are as easy as a cat in heat

Me: That offends me, I am more like a Thai whore with a drug problem!

Being sexual and playful is fine but I recommend always turning it on to her. Teasing her that she is the aggressive one looking for sex, is a great way to entertain her and make her comfortable. Don't worry I will go into this in MUCH greater detail in later chapters. However, hopefully you get it that you have to be extremely careful when talking about sex.

The Questionator

This is the insecure/nervous girl tactic. They don't have much to say themselves so they fire off one question after another. This is okay in normal conversation because most people like to talk about themselves, but in text it is irritating. Texting is a slight pain in the ass, you have to pick up the phone and hit those little buttons at about a tenth of the rate a normal conversation flows. Therefore! Don't try to use text like you would speak. Texting is fencing. You are playing together. Testing the other persons abilities and vice versa. If you sit and ask Q's all the time, the other person is going to lose interest or get a thumb cramp.

However, if she isn't responding very well to you, it certainly isn't a bad idea to end a lot of your texts with a question to encourage her to respond. But if you do this try to remember it is the guys' job to do the entertaining, which means you are being playful while asking questions.

Accepting/making last minutes dates

Texting can be a very lazy medium for both of you and it is quite easy and relatively stress free to ask you out at the last minute. Is this okay to accept?

Hmmm... I often say that, "Morality is inversely proportional to his or her hotness". In other words, the more attracted you are, the more you will accept the unacceptable. So... NO! We do not accept last minute dates because it lowers our value, and says we are at their beck and call. Last minute means the same day, the night before is acceptable as long as you make a bit of a stink about it.

I know you really want to see this girl but if she wants to meet on a whim, you really are not all that important to her. While it is cool that she is asking you out, it still is very important to make her wait and raise your value in her perception of you.

What about you asking her out at the last minute via text? This is probably been hammered into a girls head a couple of hundred times by women's magazines NOT to accept. If you do this expect a very possible "No," from her, something we really want to avoid. Always give her a couple days notice.

From FB to Texting

When I first moved back to the US, the girl that cut my hair was pretty flirtatious with me. She was cute, but being so used to Japanese girls, I was a little nervous to go out with an American girl. I was very used to texting someone before calling them so I gave her my email address. "Drop me an email sometime and let's talk," I said. She looked at me, mouth a little open as if to say, "Are you kidding me? Email?"

Like I said before, in Japan people don't text by number, they all have a separate email on their phone. So getting someone's email address was like asking for a number but FAR less intimidating. Since she didn't have email on her phone, my hairstylist had to go to a computer to drop me a line. It all worked out, but I felt a bit silly later. **Now I just use Facebook** and allow this to progress into number gathering if need be.

Do yourself a favor and use something very non-intimidating to make first contact. I love Facebook for this and since it's on my phone I can connect then and there. This is like going for a virtual coffee rather than a full date. This is the wonderful thing about FB, women are not threatened by it, and it isn't all that hard to get someone's facebook rather than a phone number.

Finally... Stop! Don't hit Send!

Your textmate is constantly assessing you, and unless they are not well-educated, they care about your spelling and grammar. Get into the habit of checking email and texts BEFORE you hit send. The last thing you want is for a girl you are interested in to think you are a moron because you said, your instead of you're. (But you can tease them a tad if they can't spell) BTW. I am horribly guilty of this so if you find any spelling mistakes in this e-book chalk it up to me wanting you to give me hell.

As a guy you probably paid less attention in English class than she did, so really take that extra little bit of time to write a better message. Her thinking you are stupid certainly isn't a positive.

Part VI - Techniques and Strategies – Building tension

Once I have broken the ice with someone and have a good dialogue going, I follow many strategies to draw them in closer. These are often very simple; like *being interesting* or more complex like *the hook*. These are the next level of tools that will allow you to get what you want from your target.

Don't be a Weenie

A reporter asked a famous quarterback, "What is the secret of your success?" The quarterback responded, "A very short memory." This means that he didn't dwell on his mistakes. He was always moving forward towards his goal and didn't apologize to anyone on the way.

I used to be the King of sorrys; constantly apologizing for who I was. You cannot do this in life, and especially not in texting. I am not talking about being late and not apologizing for it. I am talking about the incessant use of sorrys to be accepted by others. This is just ugly in text and makes you look very weak. What if instead of saying sorry you actually said, "I am pathetic, please like me" or "please accept me, I am your bitch." Would this kind of person seem attractive to you? Would you want to be friends or lovers with this person? 90% of the time, when you use "Sorry…" it is inappropriate.

This is one of the major places that men and women kill the sexual tension being created. Don't do this, take a risk and tell them to "suck it!"

Cherie: Hey Mike you going out tonight?

Me: Going out with Lacy

Cherie: Oh… going out with the cougar

Me: Jesus Cherie, you are such a bitch!

Cherie: Well she is old! Sorry was that rude?

Me: Yeah!

Cherie: Sorry about that, well call me later.

Me: I was playing with you Cherie

Cherie: Oh, sorry

Do you see? Cherie looks very, very weak here and I am actually disappointed she let me call her a bitch without coming back at me, although I could have softened it with a smiley face. Cherie could and should have done two things, set a boundary or played back. If she set a boundary she would have said, "Hey, I didn't mean to offend you but I don't enjoy being called a bitch." Ouch, I certainly would have responded to that and I would have respected her for it. OR, what she should have done was play with me. "Oh, I am a bitch huh? Do I need to come over and slap that cougar around?" HA! That would have been fun to play with and I would have enjoyed it and some attraction would have been created.

When to Text for the First Time – Resisting Impatience

I am going to contradict earlier advice right now but only for this particular instance. It is just good practice to put a little time between the first interaction and the first text.

Okay very simple and must be obeyed!!! DON'T TEXT RIGHT AWAY!! You need to wait… a minimum of a day, better yet, a few days. If it is longer than a week, I find the initial interest tends to fade. I know you really want to text them right away but this is your subconscious betraying you. This is the junk food reflex, you see something that you really want so you stuff it in your mouth and get fat. It is the same with dating; you must resist the impulse to act like an idiot. Wait a couple of days and show the other person that you are worthy of something healthy. This shows you don't want sex… immediately… in the bathroom…of a really scummy bar…

Now since very few people seem to get this, let me give you an extreme example so you will NEVER forget how important this is.

I was renovating a house in southern California and working alone. There was a knock at the door, which caused me to paint the carpet. "Shit!" I said. I opened the front door a bit irritated and was surprised by a gorgeous, petite, incredibly shapely, black girl. "Um… is this 2344 Adam? The place for rent?" she said looking at a piece of paper while I stared at her. I barely controlled the erection my eyes conveyed and said, "No… follow me." I showed her the correct place and we started to talk, and eventually I got her number. To my paint and dust covered surprise, she seemed pretty darn curious about me. "Okay, you better text me soon!" she said flashing her beautiful white teeth. Three days later I sent her a text (see I follow my own rules!!) She responded one minute later "Wow…! I thought I would never hear from you!"

We met for coffee and talked for a little while, I drove her back to her hotel and she said, "You are so cute… when are we gonna F@&#…?" My mouth dropped open and my eyes glazed. I could see all the junk food I wanted to eat. I wrestled control away from my genitals and grinned, "Sorry you are going to have to wait." I gave her a hug, a slap on the bum, and left. She texted me that night asking for my email address, and within ten minutes I got an email with an attachment. I opened it on my iPhone sitting next to a friend, "Holy crap!!" I said shooting diet coke up and out my nose. The picture was an incredibly large photo of Nina, fully nude and in a pose that only a gynecologist should see with such illumination. In the corner was her stage name Nina D### I googled her and discovered why she moved to California. She was a porn actress…

Nina had ZERO control over her Junk food impulse, she wanted sex and wanted it now! Now a lot of guys might go for this, but only once (maybe twice?) then move on. Nina got a whole lot of nothing using this approach with me. It was a HUGE turn off which showed me that she was an impatient little girl, so addicted to immediate pleasure, that she would have jumped me on the spot.

Okay, to be fair maybe this would be a turn on to many guys, but it would result in sex only and nothing concrete. As a guy you have to watch your sexual impatience, it will do nothing but scare a girl away. Nina was acting like a guy in this story and I am old enough to control my impulses. Also, by making Nina wait I drove her nuts! And it soon became her personal obsession to sleep with me. You see, having more patience than your target is a really really good thing.

Think of it this way, which roller coaster would you rather ride, the big one or the little one? The big one has a long line but the ride is so much better. The little roller coaster? Come on… only horny teenagers ride that one. Take your time and build attraction, the ride will be worth it.

(I recently got harassed on my Amazon reviews by a guy that said I was an idiot for not sleeping with this girl. Did I say I **didn't** sleep with her? Come on... remember I am a guy, and I don't easily turn down free sex from a hot girl)

"Just kidding, is the limp penis of the text world. It is soft, weak and slightly repulsive."

No Pulling Punches or JK

This is something that took me forever to learn, simply because I was so afraid of losing someone's approval. Think about how many times you have said something funny, slightly rude, to be playful but pulled it back. I know this is similar to the above section but really, you need to get this.

You know what you said... the horribly weak comment, "Just kidding." This is the limp penis of the text world. It is soft, weak and slightly repulsive. Why do you say this?? Why is nearly everything you write tempered with weak comments like "just kidding" or "sorry about that" Just cut to the chase and say, "I am really weak and I need to be approved of, so every time we interact I am going to apologize for my existence."

Jen: Hey, I just got my schedule I am free Friday and Monday

Mike: You want to go out Friday?? Don't you have a date that night?

Jen: Yeah, with you! Where are you going to take me?

Mike: Take you??? You asked Meee! I think you should be taking me out to dinner!

Jen: I only buy dinner for cute guys, not rude ones! JK

AAHHHHHHHHH!!! Did you catch that!!!??? That damn little JK at the end of the text? This is like a dinghy towed behind a yacht. Jen was doing so well too! It is as if she was pumping up the tire of interest and POW... she let all the air out with the pin of JK. What people don't understand is that JK or Sorry is very different than LOL or =). These are softeners that communicate you are playing. JK and Sorry communicates that you are weak and unsure of yourself. The last thing you want to do in text or in person.

F-ing up and Rolling with it

In all relationship interactions we need to be a Judo master. This is using the other person's power to throw them into an interesting situation. There are no mistakes, there are only opportunities!

Him: Hey Sarah, it was really nice meeting you tonight.

You: Hey Mark it was nice meeting you too.

Him: Uh, My name is not Mark.

You: Oh shit! Hahaha, well I guess the bar was a little too noisy.

Or Oops! I must have gotten one too many phone numbers last night. =)

Or That's cool my name isn't Sarah!

So what if you got their name wrong, this gives you an opportunity to roll this into something fun and interesting. Just make sure that you DON'T ruin things with uncomfortable apologies.

You see, the important thing is always portraying confidence; of course we are going to say the wrong things. Of course we are going to screw up, but if we accept this as inevitable and don't really give a shit. She will sense that confidence and feel nothing but attraction.

Purposely Misunderstanding

This is one of my favorite playful things to do. I think I learned this from being a kindergarten teacher. I would purposely misunderstand something to stimulate their little brains.

"What's this??" I yell, showing a picture to my 30 adorable 4-year old Japanese students. "It's a cat!!" they scream almost in unison, "What?? That's not a bat!!" They scream back, shaking their heads "No!!! Cat!! Cat!!" I look more confused, "a hat???" I say making the motions of putting a hat on, "No, Mike sensei!! A cat!!!" they scream, not sure how an adult can be this stupid.

This is so much fun to do; it appears totally innocent and pushes the other person to think. They have to decide if you are serious or not. If you aren't they feel a bit silly for not getting the joke and if they get it this can lead to a pretty fun banter.

Angela: Just saw Jason

Me: You're seeing Jason??? I am so hurt!

Angela: No! I just saw Jason

Me: Just saw? You mean just a fling?? We need to talk...

Angela: you dork...

This was a mild use of purposely misunderstanding but if you keep it in mind you can find tons of opportunities to use it. It is so much fun to watch someone untangle your reasoning and come back at you. This fun interaction is great at creating interest and attraction. Being witty means being intelligent, and being intelligent means being attractive.

Using but not responding to jealousy

I just had someone text me this, "OMG I am out with 8 guys right now! Where are you?"

The knee-jerk response would be to get a little jealous right? This is never a good idea. People play the jealousy card all the time but over text you have time to respond rationally to this manipulation. Never allow yourself to possess this button or allow others to push it. Texting is kick-ass practice for this particular real world interaction. Never go for this bait, it has a nasty hook in it.

What if you want to use jealousy as a tool? I have to admit I don't approve of this. Using jealousy is like kicking a rock and starting an avalanche, it can be very destructive. With that said, I still use it lightly from time to time. Usually I hide the jealousy tool by saying something that would be very hard to pick out. I also only use this as leverage over someone I am extremely attracted to. For example, the girl I currently have the hots for is only giving me one-word texts back, and it is incredibly frustrating!

Me: had a great time last night, you are pretty funny

Kristen: thanks

Me: I think you've affected my dating life

Kristen: Whys that?

Me: I want to find more cute med students to hang out with now!

Kristen: Whatever, none are as cute as me

Me: Currently rolling my eyes and making gagging sounds

Kristen: Shut up!

This jealousy was in the open but hidden at the same time. It was playful and not mean; not to mention, it worked well. Like I said before, I don't really think this is something you should do all of the time, but when you need a bit of leverage it can be effective and fun.

Let's take that original text I received above, how did I handle it?

Her: OMG, I am out with 8 guys right now! Where are you?

Me: OMG! I am at home watching Asian porn!

Her: Yuck! What is up with your yellow fever?

Me: Mind getting eye surgery, dye your hair, and wear a kimono?

Her: Snort, mind loosing five pound on that fat head of yours!

Me: Wink!

This is approximately what I said and her final comeback was pretty funny. However, I managed to kill her use of jealousy and turn it around on her in a funny way. Balance was maintained and attraction was escalated!

Always be the First to Exit the Conversation

I almost always do this and it used to be a conscious choice. I would set up a mental timer of about 10 minutes and then exit. This always ended up a teeny bit weak since I didn't really have a solid excuse. Now, I am tremendously busy, and I often don't respond to a text. This has accidently put me in control of almost every text conversation. I simply don't have time to be talking to everyone that drops me a line. My time is too valuable to spend texting all day. This sends a powerful message that I am too busy for them. I have so many things going on, so many people to talk to and if I drop you a line you are LUCKY! There is nothing worse than expressing too much need, being busy and not getting back conveys the opposite of neediness.

The Power of Silence

Another tool, greatly underestimated. People don't like silence. In fact most people get really, really uncomfortable with it. The next time you are on the phone with someone I want you to try a little experiment. It can be with anyone, family, friends, or even better, your target. The next time they tease you or say something a bit edgy, go silent for five seconds. While you are silent imagine all of the thoughts they might be shuffling. "Was that rude? Should I apologize? Is he mad at me? Is he still there?" They will probably say, "Hello?? are you still there?" but don't respond. If they ask you what your problem is, tell them something was wrong with the phone.

I know you probably won't take me up on my challenge, but I am sure you can imagine how batty people get when left with their own thoughts. This can be an amazing tool in the world of texting. For example...

Me: hey punk, what are you up to?

Her: don't call me punk, white boy!

Me: Well, with pink hair and more piercings than a hedgehog!

Her: (no response, she is not upset but she feels I deserve punishment)

Me: (still waiting but wondering if a day of waiting means you are upset with me)

Me: hey your hair isn't that pink... maybe more of a mauve...?

Her: Make me dinner and I will forgive you... bitch...

She is messing with me and I know it, I give her the upper hand because I can't put up with the silence. So I tell her that her hair is more of a mauve, but what if she still doesn't respond?? Do I...

A. Text her again?

B. Say sorry

C. Wait for her to text me back

D. Move on and text someone else.

D is definitely the best. C is okay but it leaves you a bit needy. Moving on allows me to reciprocate with silence and call her bluff. Silence is powerful and fun, don't hesitate to use it.

The Beauty of Challenge

One of the most frustrating things about meeting someone new is that they are too busy getting me to like them rather than challenging me. I call this being a social chameleon, people that blend into the background of being accepted but not really noticed. If you want to be different and be noticed you have to challenge others. This can be a bit uncomfortable but have you ever observed that some of your closest friends have started off not liking you very much? In fact, maybe you really butted heads initially? This challenge does many things, the least of which is gain respect. No one respects someone that cannot push him or her a little bit. What does this equal in text? Very simple, it means that you play and tease. You become excellent at making her work to hold her own in the conversation, for example:

Me: Coming down to see me on Saturday?

Jen: No way, you live too far away…

Me: What, you can't drive ten minutes?? Did your car break down again?

Jen: No I decided to sell it so I wouldn't be tempted to meet a guy like you.

Me: Ouch! Good one… Okay I will pick you up.

Jen: Only if you promise not to touch me!

Me: Whatever, you're the one that said… "I can't control myself when I'm with you!"

Jen: Well I was thinking about my ex boyfriend at the time.

Me: damn… what a coincidence!

Okay I think you get it… You don't have to do this all the time but be ready for it! Being a pain in the ass is a very valuable tool in your texting toolbox. We play when we can, we push boundaries and we build that attraction!

"Don't do what I have done in the past, and misunderstand shittiness for edginess; both are effective, but shittiness will backfire on you eventually."

Edginess

This is a core tool that I would like you to use whenever you meet someone new. You have been witness to this in most of my example texts and have gotten a peek at it with the challenge entry. Edginess is a step up from this; it is purposely being rough, a little mean but framed with playfulness. Is this mean or obnoxious? A stupid game?

Think about this: Who is more interesting, a friend that pushes your worldview and outright disagrees with you, or a friend that agrees with everything you say? Of course, the friend that offers challenge is oodles more interesting.

This is why so many of us are attracted to the bitch or the dick, they offer us a challenge. We look at the tattoos, piercings, and our subconscious says, "If that person fell in love with me, I certainly would be worthy!" So we chase them only to be rejected. This is not healthy for either side, but... it is perfectly acceptable to play with the human need for approval. This is not about being mean, but it's about testing our target for compatibility and strength.

Don't do what I have done in the past, and misunderstand shittiness for edginess; both work, but shittiness will backfire on you eventually. Edginess is pushing someone within the boundaries of what they can handle. Shittiness is beyond those boundaries and is hurtful.

Mike: Hey skinny! Haven't heard from you in a little while.

Chrystal: Sorry I have been busy with all the guys I am seeing

Mike: I know what you mean, too many guys in my life too! =)

Chrystal: There's a surprise, you wear too much Abercrombie to be strait

Mike: Well that is why I like you! You have the shape of a boy!

Chrystal: You asshole

Mike: wink...

This is pretty edgy and by that I mean I am really pushing the edge of what is okay to say. Chrystal got some punches in too, but I won in the end because she didn't have a good come back. After wink... I left her alone, I didn't say sorry and I didn't text her again. I won the interaction and she will have to come to me to regain balance. This is fun, she might be a tad irritated, but everyone loves a challenge.

Now, why is this not shitty or mean? Because I have not teased her about something that truly is painful. Chrystal is thin, but she is a swimsuit model and looks great. Crystal has a big nose, which I think is cute but if I was playful about this she would not take it well. It would be effective, but it might backfire on me, and I would feel like a jerk.

(The same guy that gave me such an angry review on Amazon

mentioned that I am a hypocrite by criticizing PUA's for tearing down egos, since it appears that edginess is the same thing. Not even close, edginess, like I said before is teasing but it is only over something benign. We don't make fun of something that would actually do damage. Our goal is not ego-theft; rather it is to get her to raise her sword and fence with us a bit.)

Cocky funny

I know *Challenge* and *Edginess* are incredibly similar to Cocky funny but they are such effective tools it doesn't hurt to have a little over kill. As long as you remember not to be abusive, these tools are totally appropriate to use even in long-term relationships. People love to play, and when you stop playing, you and they are bored. Boredom, is the poison of all relationships.

Remember when I said that intelligence is incredibly attractive? That is where cocky/funny falls into place and we want to be as witty as we possibly can. Then season it with a little bit of "cocky" and this will be a delicious meal few women pass up. (Girls will deny this vehemently because the last guy that failed with them didn't make her comfortable before throwing down the challenge of cocky funny)

Cocky funny has been one of the most powerful texting tools I have ever used but it is also one of the most difficult to master. Make sure that you are as cautious as possible when starting this type of interaction. If you are not used to being cocky funny you could bite off more than you can chew very very quickly. This is why texting is such a great vehicle for practicing this technique.

A couple of examples:

- I really want to meet a girl as cute as you but a little more intelligent (Dangerous, but if done at the right time with the right girl, excellent)

- I know you can be wittier than that, try again!

- I totally busted you like three times looking at my package, you know I am not a piece of meat. (Ha! Role reversal!)

Here is another example a little more on the cocky side.

Her: What are you up to tonight?

Me: Going out with YOU, impressed you had the guts to ask me

Her: Idiot, I wasn't going to ask YOU, I wanted to introduce you to my friend

Me: I like how girls who want me always push me on their friends, you shouldn't let this boyfriend thing get in the way of your obsessions

Her: May I remind you that my BF is gorgeous a 6'3" med student

Me: =) you are hot when you are angry

Her: God...

Me: Don't text me so much, it makes you seem desperate

At this point she has absolutely nothing to text and she is a little pissed. She thinks I am an arrogant ass and she hates me just a tad but this is GOOD! Now is when we sit on it a little bit and let the tension gestate.

Please understand, I honestly am not trying to steal her from her BF but I do know that she isn't happy with him and a break up is eminent. When it happens I will certainly be happy to have my rebound trampoline ready for her to bounce on all night.

Part VII - Techniques and Strategies – Escalating Sexuality

Since this is the guy's version of Textappeal I am adding a chapter on moving into the sexual. I mentioned before that sexting should be avoided, but only initially. Later, you can escalate a more sexual relationship over texting quite easily but! I recommend extreme caution. Triggering her fear response is what we want to avoid at all costs, but with skill we can turn her on and make her feel safe at the same time.

Comfort First, Then Sexual

I honestly can't count how many times a girl in my bed has said, "I don't know what it is but I am so comfortable with you, I feel like I have known you for years."

So many men thrust their sexuality on a girl like a Peter North money shot (Might be a generation gap, Google him, the guy is a geyser) You must understand that although women are sexual, they are also physically vulnerable. This means that immediate sexual aggression by you will lead to **fear, not arousal** from her. Remember, Safety THEN Sexy.

Peter: It was cool to meet you at Zodos the other night

Her: Yeah you seem pretty cool

Peter: I couldn't resist talking to you since you have such a great ass (Way too soon!)

Her: So you were checking out my ass? (She is immediately on the defensive and is setting him up for a fuck up)

Peter: Of course not, you are sexy all over

Her: What about my tits? (DANGER! DANGER!)

Peter: Fucking beautiful baby (Moron)

Her: Is that all you care about, sex? (Peter is screwed now, he can't recover from this because she has classified him as a perv and thus dangerous)

I am sure you are not an idiot like Peter, but you get the point right? Texing gives you a ton of time to think about what to say, so bloody think!

Now, the right way to get sexual:

Peter: It was cool to meet you at Zodos the other night

Her: Yeah you seem pretty cool

Peter: Seem eh? And pretty?

Her: lol, shut up you know what I meant

Peter: Well you are kinda cute and cool yourself but the booty jeans were a little tight, I think I saw way too much (sexual but not aggressive)

Her: WHAT?? Hahaha, I wouldn't be talking Mr, I look like I just walked out of a gay bar

Peter: Ah, so now you know not ALL the hot ones are married or gay

Her: I never said you were hot!

Peter: You didn't say it but you thought it

Her: So you know what I am thinking???

Peter: Yup, and no I am not going to sleep with you on the first date but I might let you kiss me.

Her: lol, what a disappointment =) and I mean the kissing!

Sooooo... much better than the first interaction. You see, by just changing your approach a little bit, massively changes the dynamic. If your intentions are to screw her, she will sense this and not be comfortable. If your intentions are to create comfort FIRST the sexual part can flow naturally. So one more time, women are JUST as horny as men but without comfort the golden vaginal gates are locked.

Using Humor to Connect Directly to the Clitoris

Humor is one of the most valuable tools you can ever master. Without the funny, cocky just looks arrogant. Without the funny, comfort is so much harder to reach. Without the funny she has to entertain you, the role of the pursuer NOT a feminine role.

Take a look at a recent comment exchange on my blog (the comment section in a blog is very similar to texting a girl). BTW I have never talked to or met this girl before.

Lindsey: hahahahahaha, damnit Mike that is so funny!! How do you answer those questions? You crack me up. **I can guarantee you get laid a lot. lol**

Mike: No comment, but it is remarkable how humor is directly attached to the clitoris. Add onto that a guy that insists on making that clitoris sing as often as possible, but once again, no comment. What are you doing later?

Lindsey: What is so humorous about the clitoris? The foreskin is funny, but I am glad you aren't singing about that.... Are you?? lol

Mike: It looks like a dirty little nun. One I want to convert.

Lindsey: Father, I doubt you could handle me nevertheless convert me

Mike: Yeah, like I haven't heard that a million times. Get on your knees, shut-up and confess, you know you will feel better. =)

Do you get this? Does this make sense to you? When you text you have a GOLDEN opportunity to connect with her sexually without having to say anything directly. Granted, above I am very sexual but I have rapport with this girl.

This means that we have an understanding, there is a balance, one that I sensed well enough to tell her to "get on your knees, shut-up and confess!" Granted I tempered it with a smiley face, as should you every time you text a girl something really edgy

Lets look at another example of using humor.

Her: So I haven't heard from you in a while

Me: Can't stop thinking about me huh?

Her: You wish, something smelled bad in the trash and I thought of you

Me: Not surprised, you are a pretty filthy girl

Her: Only in bed

Me: Yeah maybe we will have another shot at that sometime. (If you are lucky)

Her: I wanna be lucky!

Me: I used to have a dog named lucky, If you want... I still have his collar

Her: Ruff Ruff!!!

Me: I think I might have to keep you away from the cat box

Her: ROLFL, shut up! That is so gross! My dog does that all the time.

Me: Okay, lucky the dog. Beg for me and I will see you on Saturday

Her: Already on my knees =)

See how comfortable she gets with a sexual conversation when it is wrapped with humor??? I have gotten into ridiculously sexual conversations with girls I barely know because I have been able to mask it with humor. Now, that this uncomfortable sexual barrier is broken, she will be far more comfortable moving into the physical.

More Sneaking Into the Sexual

Have you ever seen a crowd of uptight white people watching a black comedian making filthy jokes? How in the world can these conservative whities be laughing hysterically about anal sex with midgets??? Because sex becomes a 1000 times more comfortable when it is funny.

Her: Why do you always date Asian girls?

Me: What, you don't know?

Her: Is it because they are submissive?

Me: No silly it is all about the plumbing

Her: What???

Me: They have small plumbing and I... well, you know...

Her: HA!! LOL are you saying you have a small dick???

Me: Like a baby, even my nuts are like pistachios

Her: LOL, killing me! You are kidding right?

Me: Why are you so obsessed with my penis?

Her: Shut up, you brought it up!

Me: Would prefer if you brought it up. You have small hands right?

Her: Hahahaha, Like a babies!

Me: PERFECT!

What do you mean you are not funny? You have hours with that bloody phone before you have to send her a text back, more than enough time to think of something. Being funny is like any skill, the more you practice it the better you get at it. Texting is the perfect place to practice this, now get on it!

6 Parts Comfort - 1 Part Sexual

In the earlier examples, there is a whole lot of sexuality in a short conversation but certainly I am not always like this. Usually I am very sparse with anything sexual, but I still like to inject the conversation periodically.

I was talking to a friend of mine the other day, who is also a dating blogger and possibly a bigger man-whore than I am. I mentioned how I like to drop sexual bombs on women totally out of the blue. He laughed and said, "Oh, you mean 6 parts comfort, 1 part sexuality?" I had never heard anyone put it into words but I realized this is exactly what I did a lot of the time. My first priority was to make her comfortable, make her laugh and then sneak in the sexuality. Most guys can't control themselves and they get the ratio bass-ackwards.

After this conversation I realized that I text the same way I talk. I tease, have fun, joke and maybe drop something slightly sexual. I use about a 6:1 ratio. Like I said before, 90% of women have a quarter of the sexual thoughts guys do. Not only that, but if you show that your intention is sexually driven it will push them away to the same extent. This doesn't mean that women aren't as horny, it only means that you MUST control yourself. If she doesn't rise to your sexual bait, it is time to change the subject.

Anna: Watcha doing tomorrow

Me: I think I am gonna watch MONSTER TRUCKS!

Anna: lol... seriously?

Me: Naw, I am going to sit at home and work on my blog

Anna: Sounds so exciting! Can I help?

Me: Sure, you are pretty smart, for a girl, but I don't feel safe being alone with you

Anna: Whatever, you wish you could be

Me: I am innocent and busy, and I am afraid you will violate me.

Anna: Dork, I am coming over.

This was interesting because the sexual roles got reversed. I made Anna into the aggressor and she fell neatly into the role. Sometimes I will be a lot more brazen and out right say something totally inappropriate, but only when the comfort is quite strong. I am insulated by the comfort and I can hit her sexual on/off switch without her caring or noticing. Fun tactic but a little advanced, be very cautious with this.

Are You Dating or F*cking Material?

This is a major mistake that many men make, they think that they need to be romantic and ultra sweet to that girl that they want to sleep with. As you may already know THIS IS A MISTAKE. Why? Because believe it or not a lot of women are totally fine with just sleeping with you. You see, if you act like relationship material you will be placed in this category and suddenly the pants become nearly super-glued on. However, if you are only about sex, she really has nothing to lose by sleeping with you.

You: Hi Sweetie, I really had fun with you last night

Her: Yeah, I hope we can go out again soon?

You: How about I cook you some dinner, I make a pretty mean curry.

Her: Wow, that sounds great, can I bring anything?

You: You provide the wine and I will provide the romance

Her: Blush, cant wait to see you.

AHhhhhhH!!!! Dude! Are you high? You just want to screw this girl, right!!?? Why the hell are you screwing with her head? Not only will it take a minimum of 5 dates to get in her pants, but when you do there will be NO WAY to get her out of the house in the morning. Next thing you know she is cooking breakfast, picking up your underwear and wondering why you keep getting so many texts from other girls! Bad move, try something like this:

You: Hey babe, little disappointed why you didn't try to kiss me last night. Most girls go for it on the first date! (This is role reversal and hinting at you having many girls)

Her: Whatever! If you wanted to make a move you should have done it

You: I am not that easy, a few girls get me into bed on the first date but it is RARE! (Again role reversal and we are steering things to something sexual, hinting at her not being good enough)

Her: If you were only so lucky to get me into bed on the first date!

You: Please... If I wanted sex I have quite a few people I could call (This communicates that you are wanted by many and very choosey, she will have a hard time replying)

Her: You are pretty full of yourself aren't you?

You: Yup, thanks for noticing, lets go out again this Thursday

Her: If you are lucky!

You: I am lucky and I will pick you up at 8

Her: fine... just don't be so damn full of yourself

You: :p

What did he do right when he text her?

- Showed he was in high demand

- Did a nice sexual role reversal

- Put her on the defensive

- Didn't apologize and created sexual tension

- Brought up the sexual without being over bearing

Excellent interaction that was fun for the girl, if they don't sleep together very soon, I will be shocked.

Please understand that a lot of my examples are extreme, in order for you to see what is possible. In no way do I expect you to do the same right out of the gate. Flirt with this type of communication first, because if you jump right in you probably won't be able to swim. Get your toes wet first, women can be sharks.

I Am a Man-Whore and You Should Stay Away From Me

This is not really so much of a texting tool as advice to this typical female concern. What I found is that it actually works WONDERFULLY in your favor to confess what you, and your typical behavior patterns are. Disclosing everything takes away any argument, or resistance she might have towards you. It seems counter intuitive, but trust me, its remarkable how well this works.

Her: So my friend told me about you

Me: Oh really? Was it about me stealing from homeless children?

Her: Haha, No, he said that you sleep with every girl you meet (Most likely it is a guy trying to cock block, Asshole...)

Me: Oh really, yeah that is probably true, I need to stay away from the local geriatrics home. Gets me in trouble (jUDo! cHOp!)

Her: Nasty! So it is true?

Me: I don't feel guilty about enjoying sex since I am very honest with people. I don't cheat, I don't lie, so what is the problem?

Her: Yeah, you seem cool, I think my friend is just jealous

Me: Sounds like it, but take his concern to heart and be careful around me. Next thing you know you will be naked and liking it

Her: Ha! Maybe I should stay away from you! =)

Do you see that rolling with the cock blocker's sabotage really worked to my benefit? Do you see how she reacted? I moved from relationship material to sex material, which is certainly a good thing. Also there is now a challenge; every woman wants to be the one that catches the guy no other woman could. How cool is that??? I can be totally honest and at the same time have women go out of their way to sleep with me!!

To be fair though, this is no longer my agenda, but I will still be dead honest. The point is that you should not have to lie to seek out approval.

Almost always, honesty works in your favor, girls aren't stupid and they will smell a dishonest guy 50 feet away.

Never Have a Sexually Based Agenda

When you focus on creating comfort, rather than getting laid, you are far far more likely to get laid. You have essentially removed the largest obstacle besides her jeans. However, this is something that you cannot fake, in other words if your agenda is to get laid it will shine through no matter how you try to hide it.

Her: So my friend tells me that you are a bit of a player

Him: If you mean that I have slept with a lot of people, yes. Is my agenda to get laid? No.

Her: Bullshit, It is every man's agenda to get laid!

Him: I love sex, I adore women but just like everyone else, I want to meet a great girl and have great sex on top of that

Her: So you are saying that you don't want to sleep with me *rolls eyes*

Him: Of course I would, but that is not what drives me. I would rather see if we have a connection first (YES!! Home run right here)

Her: I get that, I just don't want to be used

Him: =) If it makes you feel better I will let you use me instead, gotta go to work TTYL

This text exchange was pure Judo on his part. **He agreed with nearly every thing she said and turned it into a point for himself.** However, he couldn't have done this if it weren't really true. This guy is comfortable with his promiscuity, he doesn't lie about enjoying sex, and it makes his statement very honest. Sure there might not be a connection between them but because he is so honest with his intentions she will be totally comfortable to give him a shot.

I want to add one more thing, notice he never disagrees with her? Do you see how it moves her in his direction? Improv comedy has really only one rule, never disagree with the other comedian. Why? Because it will halt the sketch in it's tracks by killing the momentum. This works the same with a woman, and if she says something like, "I don't think I should come to your house yet". You say, "I totally understand, I would probably feel it is too soon as well." This takes all the pressure off and gives her control over the situation. Strangely enough though, she will probably end up at your house because you were fine with her not. (Yes women are a bit insane)

Part VIII - Techniques and Strategies – Maintaining balance

"One more rule that you are NOT allowed to break: If you receive a text you can send a text, never send multiple texts if he or she has not responded yet."

Get a Text - Give a Text

Now that you know not to contact her right away, what happens after you make first contact? Is it okay to text anytime? Do you text her at 8 in the morning? "Good morning sexy, so glad to have met you," or maybe you send her four chatty texts in a row just to keep her attention? Sounds reasonable?

NO!!!! One more rule that you are NOT allowed to break! If you receive a text you can send a text. Never send multiple texts if she has not responded yet! Later we can bend this rule a teeny weensy bit but for now you must stick to the rule… Seriously! I know better than you on this subject. Don't think this is okay to bend this rule.

Just to let you know how serious I am about this I am currently following my own rules. I often bend them but at the moment I am emotionally compromised and in my temporarily insane state, I need rules. I have been seeing on and off a gorgeous girl that works at a bookstore. She is SO cute that my junk food impulse is off the scale. I can't tell you how much I want to call, text, or visit her store. She is killing me with this couple-month long foreplay!! Why don't I just give in and text her?

THE ONLY REASON SHE IS STILL INTERESTED IN ME IS BECAUSE I AM NOT GOING AFTER HER. If she does not return a text I don't try again. She has the emotional upper hand, she knows I am goo goo for her, but she is baffled by my self-control and she won't give up until she breaks it. Thank God I have rules! The last thing I want is to get needy and screw up the balance.

Her: Sorry, can't talk right now, get back to you soon!

You: Hey that's cool, just wanted to say hi!

You: Did you know that there is a new theater near my house?

You: I want to see the new Batman, do you have time on Sat?

You: Wow... you really are busy!

How do you think she is going to feel when she picks up her phone and sees four texts? Or what if she keeps seeing these texts coming in and she starts feeling a level of irritation. Remember the Teeter Totter!? What are you doing to it right now? You are jumping up and down on it like a baby kangaroo on crack, and this will only irritate the crap out of her. Get a text – Give a text, no exceptions (Long term couples can benefit from this too, but of course we can be a lot more lenient)

The Art of Push and Pull

Push and pull I have heard in the PUA world many times but I have never heard a good explanation as to why it works, and I have never heard it applied to texting. What I didn't realize, is that I use it all the time unconsciously, and it works beautifully in the texting medium.

I liken push and pull to self-stimulation (you get what I mean, right?) as you "work" on yourself, you are creating arousal. If you only "pulled" or only "pushed" there would be no "erecting" attraction and certainly no release. In the texting world it might look like this:

You: Hey cutie, did you get that job yet? (pull)

Her: Don't know yet kinda worried

You: Well, if you weren't so under qualified (push)

Her: Hey! What's that supposed to mean!?

You: I was talking about us (second push)

Her: Whatever, you wish you could date me! =)

You: Sigh, you are right, I am certainly not in your league (pull)

Her: Gawd! Whatever... you are so full of yourself

You: Sure am, and that's why you have the hots for me (push)

Her: hahaha, not...

You: Okay sweetie, got to run, good luck on the job and let me know if you get it (pull)

Her: Thanks! Take care...

We have just stimulated the situation and because there was no release we have built up the interest for the second interaction, nicely done.

(Let me add something, just read another "textpert's" advice on how to text women. To my lack of surprise, it was relatively rude and about 90% push. This is a very common mistake, the guy doesn't incorporate enough push and puts himself at risk of being labeled an ass, or only creates attraction based on temporary negative tension. You don't have to be a dick to stimulate attraction, rather just cool and playful.)

Keeping the Target Off Balance

When I was in nutrition school I remember reading about a fascinating study involving rats. If I remember right, there were two groups of rats, one group would push the lever 5 times and get a treat. The other group would receive a treat at very random intervals, for example, 1 push, or 23 pushes of the lever. Here is the really interesting part, one group became neurotic and obese. Which one? You would think the group that received a predictable feeding, but they were quite normal. The erratic feedings did something very strange to the rats; it made the food unpredictable and thus more precious. Those little buggers would push that lever all day long and eat as much as they could.

Is your target as simple as a rat? Absolutely! Of course we don't want her to become neurotic over you, but we certainly increase interest by not being predictable. How does this apply to text?

- Don't text her every night before bed, break it up, keep her wondering.

- Don't ask her the same questions, or tell her about your day, everyday, boring...

- Space out your responses, wait a min, or a day, shake it up

- Don't say yes so much, throw in a few no's to her desires.

- Send a long text, send a short one, or don't respond.

Point is that John Doe is too safe and not interesting. Being erratic and hard to read is a wonderful way to build curiosity. You goal is to hear her say, "You are so interesting, I just can't figure you out." YES, this is what we want, to be different, special and therefore, attractive.

Giving Power

I remember when I just met a really pretty Japanese girl in Japan. At the time my Japanese was pretty bad and her English was not too great. I thought she was a knockout and didn't have a chance with her so I teased her a bit too much over text. What came back humbled me, and I realized I was not sensing the power balance very well.

Sayuri: Mike you very nice guy. I need get to know but I am very insecurity.

This is when I realized that I had taken things a little bit too far and I had to tone things down a bit and give some power back. What was my response?

Me: Thank you for your text Sayuri. I think you are very sweet and pretty. I want to know you too.

I didn't apologize or say sorry I only matched her vulnerability. I realized I came on too strong initially and backed down. Be challenging but be sensitive to the balance. In the beginning, I experienced many painful rejections because I thought I needed to pound a tack with a sledgehammer.

Using Softeners

This is a pretty large part of texting in other countries, but lacking in the States. The use of emotional indicators like =) or "LOL." In other countries, these are called emoticons (emotion icons) and are similar to IM. I really like emoticons and hope that more people start to use them! They really help in understanding the difficulty of expressing tone in text. Here are some old school examples of Japanese emoticons. They are so fricken cool!!

55

(*_*) o(^-^)o (^O^)/ (>_<) (-_-) (?_?) (^^ (´Д`) (UoU)

w(° °)w (_ _)Zzz \(^^) (-_-)

Aren't those killer!!?? I use a few of them in text, but I usually use them in emails. I keep a copy on hand to slip them in here or there for nauseating cuteness. Good stuff! I think in the next year or two because of the iPhone we will see a leap in texting technology. If not, I am going back to Asia.

P.S. Just got Emoji set up on my iPhone, these are little faces just like ones you see on IM, for the moment they can only be received by certain phones. There are multiple apps in the app store that activate this Japanese function on your phone. Just type in Emoji in the search bar of the app store.

Okay, back to the point. Using things like emoticons and explainers like LOL (laugh out loud) LMAO (Laughing my ass off) really help to set tone in a text. Sometimes I just say "wink" or "rolling eyes" in line with a text.

Why use these?? They allow your original meaning to be well understood and to stop anyone from taking you too seriously. I personally find the use of the simple happy face to be more than effective at making it clear you were not trying to be a jerk but you just want to play. =)

When helping my buddy get the attention of a girl, I made a very simple text that made all the difference with a smiley face.

Ben: Hey I know you're mad at me right now but if you don't get back to me I will be forced to slip into a deep depression. =)

This communicated playfulness well, without it the text could have been taken a bit too seriously. Use these softeners if tone is in doubt or just for the hell of it.

Word of caution, DON'T OVER USE LOL AND =) If you do they will lose their effectiveness. There is a girl on Twitter that does this to me, and it becomes like an obnoxious giggle; no substance, just space filler. Here is an example of how **not** to use softeners and explainers.

"LOL weak ego? NOT at all. LOL I'm just really proud of my body! Took me a long time to get here and now I'm all about showin off. LOL"

She used these pretty much in every sentence! And it is almost as obnoxious as me using exclamation points all the time!!! OR TYPING IN CAPS ALL THE TIME!!!

Getting her to commit to the date

Frustrating isn't it? When she says that he wants to go out but is all mushy on the time, place, and date. When I was working as a nutritionist/personal trainer I gained the skill of nailing people down to their intentions, and let me tell you, this is a skill! But once aware, mastery takes no time.

Jen: Hey Ben, sorry I didn't text you back last night went to bed early. So yes I would be interested in going out sometime

Ben: Great, what day are you free?

Jen: Free on Friday night

Ben: Cool, pick you up at 8, and does Italian food sound good?

Jen: Make it 7 and you have a deal =)

Ben: 7 it is, see you soon.

Do you see how quickly Ben when in for the kill when Jen mentioned a vague, "I would be interested in going out sometime". If you have a flaky woman on your hands, or a girl that doesn't seem as interested. You have to be assertive to nail her down to a date. You see, so often the girl needs your encouragement for that first date because she is nervous. Once the date is over, she suddenly is a thousand times more comfortable with you. And all it took was for you to seal the date and not give her an opportunity to be a flake.

Jen: Hey Ben, sorry I didn't text you back last night went to bed early. So yes I would be interested in going out **sometime**

Ben: That's cool, let me know when is good for you. =)

Jen: Okay, not sure pretty busy this week

Ben: No worries, I can wait

Jen: You are so sweet, hey I have to go, my friends are here

Ben: Okay cutie, have a good night

Dude… What are you doing? Do you need a tampon? Why are you such a wuss here? Ben just got walked on by being a "nice guy" and allowing Jen to control the situation. You see, what Jen really wants is a guy that is going to be assertive, be aggressive, and take the lead. Being a passive guy waiting for her to make the move because you are afraid of rejection pretty much guarantees it.

Setting Powerful Boundaries

Setting boundaries is possibly the most critical tool for relationship success. I learned this lesson from teaching children and was shocked that it applied so strongly to male/female interactions.

When I was a kindergarten teacher in Japan, I wanted to be that one teacher they never forgot. That rockin', killer, fun teacher that everyone loved. I still painfully remember my second week of teaching when one of my students ran up to me, angry about an activity and… SPIT ON ME!

I downed two beers on the train ride home feeling so depressed that I couldn't control a bloody class of Japanese five year olds! What in the world was I missing? The next day I came into class mildly hung over and totally burnt out. I didn't give a smelly crap what these kids thought of me. "Keisuke, SIT DOWN!" I yelled and pointed at the floor, the class went silent.

It took a little time but later I became that teacher that the children adored and would remember for a lifetime. How? Well it started with not needing their approval. I didn't need them to be happy and I was fine with one or all of the little buggers hating me. I did my job, I did it well, and I was kind but strict.

There is no 100% approval, it cannot be found, as every president of the US has discovered. There are some people that are not going to like you and there are some people not worth liking. However, amazingly, when you clearly don't give a damn, and are not looking for approval, things flip and everyone seeks your approval instead. Which of course you may or may not conditionally give.

Her: Hey Jim, so sorry but that date we had planned? I can't go, I have to much work.

Jim: Really? This will be the second time that you have cancelled on me and with only one-day notice?

Her: So sorry, I will make it up to you!

Jim: Honestly, I don't know if I want you to. Now I have to make new plans. Is your time more valuable than mine?

Her: Okay, now I feel guilty

Jim: I honestly am not trying to punish you, but changing on me last minute isn't cool.

Her: Hey, tell you what, let me move things around and keep that date.

Jim: I would appreciate that

This girl is attempting to squirm out of a date with Jim, now the typical response would be to let her. This is a great time to do something counter intuitive and build the sexual tension. Sure you are taking a risk, but you must do this in order for her to respect you. Constantly allowing a woman to get away with poor behavior shows you are weak, and encourages her to be even more shitty in the future.

Setting boundaries in a relationship is the same is setting boundaries of self-respect. With my students I sacrificed my self-respect out of a need to be liked by them. So what did they do? They looked to see how far they could push it, and NO ONE is an exception to this, hell even my ten pound pet pig will charge at people in order to establish dominance (yes, I have a pet pig) if someone runs from him, he will give chase, but if you stamp your foot and say, "NO!" you have just set a boundary, and Frankie will back down. Everyone pushes everyone, but the critical part is to have enough strength to say "NO!" even if it is to my mini pig.

Him: Hey sexy, been thinking about you all day

Her: Really? What have you been thinking about, my stellar

personality!?

Him: Actually, your fantastic ass

Her: Thanks?

Him: Go to the mirror and send me a picture

Her: Jay, how do I say this. Um… I don't really enjoy when you talk about sex all the time. I like you but we are not involved enough for me to accept this.

Him: Oh hey, I was just playing. But you do have a great butt!

Her: Jay, I am serious.

Him: Sorry =) I will focus on your stellar personality next time.

her: Thanks =)

This is a great example of a girl setting an excellent boundary with a guy. She does it nicely without anger, and he respects her for it. Setting boundaries is something we have to constantly do with friends, family, and girls. There is a trick to this though, first, you need to know exactly where your boundary lies, and second, anger never enters a boundary conversation. Anger will stimulate emotion from her and that emotion will probably be quite negative.

Setting the Pace

You know when you send a text and get one back so fast that you can't put it away? You take a look only to see it is from the girl you just sent a text to. You send another and bam! Not ten seconds later there's a response. Wow… is she just holding her phone, looking at the clock and waiting for my next text? That is a little bit creepy (needy). You decide to put the phone in your pocket and get back to her after you have plucked your nose hair and… eventually forget.

If she had waited, rather than hanging on your every word, maybe you would have responded. A very simple rule to keep you safe is to follow her pace. If she takes five minutes to get back to you, DO THE SAME… Better yet if she takes five, you take ten. If you can set the pace this means that she is the one waiting for you. Maybe they won't notice consciously but it will make a difference. She might wonder deep down why you don't seem quite as interested as she is, and she will try harder. This is subtle but don't underestimate it.

Word of warning, don't overdo this! We need to keep some excitement going and if you are making her wait a day to three before responding, she very well might move on. Match her interest but be slightly behind her, this is the secret.

Part VIIII - Techniques and Strategies – Getting their attention

Whether it is reopening a conversation or talking for the first time there are a lot of ways to screw up. The number one problem is looking too interested and ruining the balance. I want you to sneak in under her radar, and become a part of her life effortlessly.

Using Facebook

Remember before when I talked about using FB to get a girl on the line? Well FB f-ing rocks nearly as much as texting. Asking for her FB is an excellent way to make a connection, without looking needy. As a guy, asking for a phone number is something we generally dread. This is what makes facebook so nice, girls don't find it nearly as intimidating as handing out their phone number. You can't take back giving a number, but you can unfriend someone on FB with one click.

Getting someone's FB is really quite effortless, all you need to do is come across as safe. In other words you are getting their FB in order to be friends and nothing else. Sure you could have the worst intentions at heart, nasty porno sex, involving vegetables, but she doesn't need to know that. Just remember that you collect people FB's all the time, and all you have to do is act the same way you might with the same sex. "Hey, you are pretty interesting, lets stay in contact over FB?" Then you whip out your iPhone and add her then and there.

Once on FB you can start the flirtation process, and see how she responds. Eventually, you should move her to text and finally to phone. Always start with the safest medium and move up from there.

Please remember again how important it is to make her feel physically safe. Asking for her phone number, where she lives, who she lives with, or where she works, just freaks women out. Keep it safe and use FB to increase her comfort with you.

The Accidental Text

One of my readers actually gave me this idea and I think it is a cute way to get a girls attention again.

You: She was so nasty!

Target: What???

You: Oh shit, that was supposed to go to someone else! But hey, how are things?

Target: lol, no problem, things are good

You: Great, hey listen, I am meeting some friends at Vasco's on Friday. Care to join us?

Target: Okay, sounds like fun

You: Killer, I will text you on Friday to let you know the time.

Target: Looking forward to it =)

This is a great way to open up a stagnant conversation without looking needy. All you did was "make a mistake" and it got her back into interacting with you. Make sure though that your mistake is funny and makes her curiosity scream. Once she is talking to you, start up the fun banter, and if she has been elusive, take the chance to ask them out to something non-threatening, like a party, bar with friends, coffee shop, easy right?

Here are some more examples of accidental texts:

Are you serious?

I think she is bi...

They took everything!

It was so disgusting, I had to wash my face.

It isn't that expensive, lets just go to Vegas and do it!

The idea is to have something "slip-out" that is from a conversation with a friend. All you have to do is hook her interest, and she will **have** to respond.

"All you need to do is give them a good reason to want to talk to you. Create this by providing them with something they really want to know about; which you, as the gatekeeper, don't divulge easily."

The Hook

The Hook is one of my favorite techniques; it is powerful but needs to be used very sparingly. It is used primarily to get someone's attention who is not reciprocating. It really should only be used once in a GREAT while or it will be seen through and you will be discarded. The hook is up there with Jealousy because it flirts with dishonesty and no one wants to be dishonest. This is how it works, you have someone that is not contacting you or texting you back and you want to jump-start a conversation with them again. All you need to do is give them a good reason to want to talk to you. Create this by providing them with something they really want to know about, which you, as the gatekeeper, don't divulge easily.

Jen: Hey Mike... have not talked to you in a bit. Just heard something very interesting about you.

Me: Hey, what did you hear??

(People are very narcissistic and crave to know what others think of them. I know it is tempting to feed them something but I want you to resist.)

Jen: What are you doing Friday? There is a get together at Fathom and your buddy Jake is going

Me: Jake, how do you know Jake? Yeah I might go... What did you hear?

Jen: Hey I have to go but maybe I will see you Friday...

Me: K let me think about it

Jen did everything right here. She played a hook and she set a little jealousy bait. Mike didn't realize Jen knew Jake and he is slightly concerned. He is also drawn to the party in order to hear what she heard. She played this well by ducking out of the conversation and avoiding answering. This means that if Mike wants an answer he has to go to the party. Here is the interesting thing, Jen may never tell Mike what she heard and Mike might not even care. The interest Mike had for the information is now transferred to Jen and it becomes unnecessary (If not a mistake) to tell him at this point. If he pushes you though, make sure you have something cute to say. Like, "My sister saw you at Ralphs and thinks you have a cute butt, I set her strait."

Here are some examples of hooks:

"Just had a dream about you"

"Just ran into your ex"

"A friend told me something pretty funny about you"

"I found and old photo of you"

"I was thinking about you today and couldn't stop laughing!"

(Just had a dream about you is a pretty funny one. Most people love to hear this kind of thing; it feeds their ego like you wouldn't believe. A fun twist on that is once you confess the dream you might make it very unflattering. Tell them something like, "You were running around work naked and your butt was jiggling like two balloons and then one popped!!" I know it makes no sense but what dream does?)

Encouraging Her to Answer

Is she not answering as fast as you would like? Could this possibly be because you are boring as hell?

Him: Hey cutie whatcha doin'?

Her: Working on a report

Him: Sounds fun =)

Her: not really

Him: Busy this weekend?

Her: Yeah a little bit

Him: Cool, talk to you later.

Ah… ouch, please remember that as the man you are the entertainer, you can't allow your target to get away without a couple laughs at least. This incredibly boring interaction, is killing his chances. Not only that but none of his texts are encouraging her to answer, in fact he is actually setting himself up for rejection.

Him: Hey cutie whatcha doin'?

Her: A report for work =(

Him: Really? And is that why you had the time to post ten more pictures of you and your bunny on facebook??

Her: Hey! My bunny is cute and unlike you. I at least keep my shirt on in my profile pics.

Him: Well, I probably look better with my shirt off, you busy this weekend?

Her: My ass, you look better with your shirt off! And I have no plans this weekend.

Him: Well I look forward to some shirtless FB profile pics. :p You up for a movie this Sat?

Her: Why not but keep your shirt on.

Him: You too, that's something I just don't need to see

Her: Shut up

Do you see how much more fun this was??? She wanted to answer him because he was so edgy and funny. He was **so** challenging that she was forced to answer him. He also encouraged a response by dropping a few questions, and even better, these questions led to a date.

Emergency! Damage Control

Since I wrote TextAppeal I have been inundated with emails in the Emergency/Damage control category. Readers realized that they have made a major mistake texting or in person and they have no idea how to rectify the situation.

Unfortunately, as I explained earlier, this is a very difficult situation to salvage because the balance is horribly compromised. But, since this might have been the reason you bought this book, I clearly don't want you to give up!

Once the balance is damaged it is very hard to regain and usually you only have a 50/50 chance of getting it back. Even for me this is a huge challenge, but since I have made these mistakes often, I very rarely make them again. Most of the time you are going to have to take your lumps and write this situation off to a learning experience.

So let's review what you probably did to make them go AWOL

- You texted multiple times without a response – Fastest way to permanently slam the door with your target. This is the number one mistake, and the easiest to avoid.

- You were overly sexual – Guys, not safe not smart, and it is just freaking her out. Do yourself a favor and jerk off BEFORE you text her.

- You went Emo – Showing your emotions too soon by sending a text like, "Are you still seeing your ex??" or "I think you are a cool girl and I want to know what this means" is something that will only shoot you in the ass. Instead, allow her show her feelings a bit first before you take the next step. (Remember the body builder!)

- Pack your bags, we're going on a guilt trip! – This happens to me constantly when I don't respond soon enough, say the "right" thing, or reciprocate feelings. I get something like, "I see that you are too busy to talk to me, well... have a nice life with whoever you are seeing now." This only makes people want to do one thing, slam the door.

- You demanded or hinted at (sexual) exclusivity – Saying something like "I took my profile down from match.com," sounds innocent enough but unless your target hints or says it first, don't make this move. This is needy and can only be done if you are 100% sure your target reciprocates your feelings.

- You demanded a certain relationship/situation outcome – Just had a girl get really upset with me because I refused to meet her for coffee. She had an emotional investment in me and like a petulant child, threw a tantrum when she didn't get what she wanted. This type of reaction is ugly and nearly impossible to recover from. Control yourself, you are no longer 10.

The reason I am repeating some of these trigger points is because you may not know why that person turned tail and disappeared. If one of these strikes a cord hopefully the pain of losing the other person's attention is sufficient punishment to learn from!

Now, how do we fix things? Whew… this is like climbing a tree backwards but it is possible. Here are a couple of questions I have received from readers that might speak to your situation.

A few emergency questions from readers

Dear Mike,

Jack and I met at a party and we hit it off immediately. The second time we met up we had sex (too early?) We started spending more time together and I started to fall for him. I was the first person to say I love you and I think I killed the balance.

After I said that, Jack backed off and it broke my heart. I usually don't rush into things like this and I feel so stupid. I still see Jack because we are in the same biking club. Recently I went biking with another guy and I think he got a bit jealous since he asked about the other guy over a text.

What do I do? We still talk over text but I don't know what to say. Is there any way I can get him back over text? How do I handle the awkwardness I feel when I see him in my biking group? Should I just move on, or do I still have a chance?

Thanks, Linda

Ouch...

Glad you heard the message on balance, but it sounds like the teeter-totter got seriously rocked. There is an expression in the dating community, "The person that cares least wins." I would like to add more to that, "The person that **appears** to care the least wins." That means that you didn't bring your poker face and you trashed the game. Now he no longer wants to play. How do you regain this? All you have to do is convince him that you are a worthy opponent again! but alas... that is really f-ing hard to do.

Can you do this over text? Absolutely! But these situations are very, very hard to salvage even for me, so I would probably have to coach you through it and I do charge for that. However, if you want to give it a run on your own do this:

- Work the jealousy angle without being obvious (His inner gorilla will want to reclaim what he thinks is his)

- Embrace the biking together and show ZERO awkwardness (This will make him feel safe)

- Become playful again and hint at a little sexuality (One thing that women can do that men can't, his penis is pretty easy to control but once you have him sexually again it is time to prove that you are a worthy adversary)

- Keep dating other men (Nothing works better to keep you emotionally insulated and improve your poker face)

Good luck...

Mike

Later I got a rather angry email back from her. The email was basically, *"So I have to play fucking games to get him back!!?? He is not a friend but an adversary??"*

Sigh... I will someday write my magnum opus on this question. Here is how I responded to her.

You seem very resistant to any kind of "manipulative" tactics to regain his attention and I don't wish to write a long email to non-receptive ears.

If you want his attention again, there are no other tactics that will work as well. Attraction is very much based in the primitive mind and this animal mind responds very, very well to simple concepts every good sales person excels at. You feel that it is dishonest to expand the truth a bit, but I am telling you not only will it work, but it will be appreciated.

Use these things only to bring him back into your orbit and discard later.

The sale needs to be made, and a little bit of puffering will not hurt as long as the product is good.

The next question is from a gay man who hired me for consultation. I really wanted to include this to show you that it really doesn't matter if you are gay straight or bi, male or female, nearly every thing works the same for everyone. Pay attention here since Dennis makes about every mistake possible.

Correspondence with Dennis and his target:

Him: Hey boy, Can we take a raincheck for tonight? I gotta run some errands, then gym at 6 and then dinner at my friend's. Sorry. I can do Thursday after 5.

Sounds like he is already having second thoughts?

Me: Yeah. I work til 730 Thursday. 730 work?

Him: I have a birthday party to go at 9. But I can grab coffee before that. At 7ish.

Me: Can't make it by 7, work til 7:30. I'm off Friday and weekends.

Him: Ok, let's do Friday. I might work during day, but if I don't I'm off all day.

Me: Ok. That's works. Just let me know what time works for u.

This sounds awfully bland, why aren't you playing with him more? I would have given him hell about breaking a date. Next time this happens make him kiss the ugliest mole you possess, or worse...

Next Day:

Me: What's up champ? I either saw u or ur twin on 23rd?

Notice you were the first to contact again, you can't do that. You were the last to mail the night before but you added a decent hook to get him interested. Once again where is the banter? Champ? He needs a nickname that is a little playful and/or mildly unflattering. For example: "What's up dimples??"

Him: I was just on 8th ave and 21st. But I didn't go to 23rd. That'd be my twin

Me: So what's the plan tomorrow? Early dinner? Daytime? Need to plan schedule a few other things.

Bland!!! You are being too cautious and the fact that he isn't bantering back shows a lack of interest. How about, "Your twin?? Yeah I thought he looked a bit cuter but don't worry you have a nicer ass" This is a back handed complement, something you should be handing out like the shiners do flowers.

Me: Btw- I was just too popular on grindr and had to delete it. (JK- I did delete it though).

(Note: we have met several times in the past in person, but he messaged me on grindr - a personals gay app on iphone. He pursued me at first and asked me out. He said he had always thought I was hot. I said the same about him.)

Him asking you out is a good sign, but you text him twice in a row again. (Edited out) AND you said JK. What you communicated to him by saying you deleted yourself from grinder is that you are demanding commitment, AND that you really weren't that popular on grindr. That isn't attractive, is it? You have only met him once for coffee and you are already looking for commitment? I can feel a bit of concern building.

Him: I'd say lunch tomorrow? I bet u were popular. Lol

Okay, good answer on his part maybe he didn't pick up you trashing yourself.

Me: Lol. Nah. Lunch it is. Whats Ur preference? How's Mexican? Let's say 1 o'clock?

Buuuuu... (Sound of the wrong answer on jeopardy) Lol NAH!?? No!!! you are the hottest thing since Lady Gaga showed her fake package on youtube! Next time you answer, "Hell yeah I am, good luck keeping me, with these looks and my unbelievable sexual prowess, I'm a bit in demand!"

Next Day:

Me: Enjoying this weather? ;(How about rosa mexicana tom on 18th and bet 5th and bdwy?)

You starting the conversation every time is like paying for dinner every time. You never allow the other person to express their appreciation for you.

(A few more texts went back and forth but not very animated, basically the target seems to worm out of another date. The next text my client shows frustration and really buries himself)

Me: You had mentioned that. I may make other plans tomorrow then. I'm gonna level with u cause Life is way too short. Ur very easy to talk to and I would like to know u more. It also helps that ur very cute with amazing eyes. If u wanna get together again, great- if not I get it. Your a cool guy.

So there has been silence since my last text above. It sounded bitchy (my text).

Help and advice please!!! I suck at dating and the texting thing. It never gets easier.

Thanks,

Dennis

He is sending a lot of mixed messages here, often he responds as if he is reciprocating your feelings but he doesn't take the effort to tell you first.

He is always one step behind you but this is very much your fault since you are awfully needy. Paying attention to these details is incredibly crucial in the courting stage because it is the time that attraction and sexual tension is laid down. But, of course you know all of this and you just want him back paying attention to you.

Attraction is like tennis; if both players are not equally skilled it isn't fun for either of them. You communicated that you were not his equal in tennis and he quickly decided he didn't want to play.

The trick to getting him back on the line is giving him a little bit of time to forget his mild discomfort, and then show him that you are as good a tennis player if not better. Then once he is back you make sure that you are under control!

Your final text really wasn't as bad as you might think although giving an ultimatum on attraction never really works. It is more of a way to self-sabotage so you can prove to yourself he wasn't interested in the first place.

We are going to wait about a week, and then I want you to send him a text that gets him talking again. You could use the hook, but that may not work since you already said way too much. Rather, I want you to send something disarming and funny. It has to fit with your personality so feel free to tweak my suggestions but please check with me before you hit send.

Something like this will work:

- So I jumped back on Grindr to find your twin but unfortunately he was way too attracted to me and I had to let him go. =) How's life cutie?

- You wouldn't believe it but my phone was crushed by a taxi last week and I couldn't receive any texts! but I am sure I missed a ton from you. Lol… What's new?

The idea is to brush off what you said last and allow him to give you a fresh start. This can only be done if you show that you don't care about his lack of response, which will put him at ease, and allow him to feel comfortable with giving you a second chance. Basically, you ignore any past interaction and bring on your "A" game from this point on.

Play with the responses above, tweak one to your needs and send it one week later at a time when you know he is free (not in the morning). Then... hold your breath. It is a last ditch attempt, once the ship is sinking it is awfully hard to save it.

Good luck Dennis and keep me posted.

Dennis did exactly what I said and it did work, he got his target back on the line but unfortunately, he wasn't able to keep the dialogue interesting enough to keep his fish.

When you get the fish back on the line you must, must, must bring your A game, you must send exceptional texts, be playful, be a pain in the ass, wait to reply, and PLEASE leave the conversation first. (I might leave the conversation first after a day of interaction and then wait two or three days to initiate contact again, this proves you are safe and not going to be a force five clinger)

Hey Mike,

Here's the deal. I met this girl, Heather on the Internet and we've been texting back and forth for a few weeks now. The first week was great, as we got to know each other. But last weekend, she didn't respond to some of my texts. I want to meet her for coffee but it seems kind of tough to get her responding. I don't want to come across as needy so I only message her a few times a week and she does not respond. Mike I feel stuck. HELP!! I don't want to blow it with her.

Have you met her in person?

No, I have not. We talked about meeting for coffee which she never went through with. But I'm not a quitter and I think I can regain some ground. I texted her an open loop question to which she did not respond. At this point, I just want her to be receptive again.

So what do you think? Can cocky and funny texts help with getting out of the "damage control stage?" Should I let it go and move on? I hate to give up so easily. I would be happy to pay for your services.

-Jackson

I hate to say it but I think you have already lost this one, and the fact that you have never met makes me even more sure. You are beyond damage control at this point and all you are doing right now is coming across as creepy.

I am a big fan of being a quitter, learn the lesson and move on!

I assume that you already purchased my book and that is why you know I charge for longer answers but I can't in good conscience charge you for this. I would be happy to coach you through another situation but this is something that no amount of wit can help with. It seems you have triggered her fear response and any pushing will only make it worse.

Of course I am going off of what you are telling me and if I understand it right you have sent her multiple texts with no response from her. If that is the case, then the door is closed on this one.

The only other option is waiting a week or two and using "the hook" or some really killer banter to get her interested again.

Wish I could give you a better answer.

Good luck

Mike

Thank you for the response, I appreciate it. I think I'm going to wait a week or two. Could you help with an example of some killer banter or a good hook? If that doesn't work, then I'm done.

-Jackson

No problem, so often even if a situation could be salvaged you really don't want to go through the effort of trying to. It simply isn't worth it. I would compare it to losing a job and begging and pleading for it back. Wouldn't it be better just to start fresh?

I would really like you to take this to heart for the next interaction, you must not pursue too aggressively. This is why I wanted you to get Ignore and Score, Bob covers the topic of push and pull very well. Push and pull is the basis for all interactions with your target, and is the reason why cocky funny works well. This is also the reason why you lost this fish, you were all pull, no push.

So after about a week, you can go for one more shot. Since her defenses are probably up, you need to make her feel safe. Send her something that communicates you don't need her, you don't want her, and she is safe talking to you.

What to say to rekindle the conversation and appear safe? Tough one since I don't know what you've talked about in the past.

But let's give it a shot, how about:

So I haven't heard from you in about a week, and I got so depressed that I jumped off my roof to kill myself. Unfortunately, I live in a tent and it didn't work out to well. =) So how are things?

This makes light of your interest in her and is disarming; she will probably open the door a crack to this.

Good luck buddy, let me know how things work out.

She ended up responding to the above example and they started up a dialogue again. Interestingly, Jackson ended up losing interest after meeting her for coffee. Which is exactly why you should NEVER build up a crazy fantasy in your head over someone you have never met. I don't care if they have 1000 FB photos and you have skype sex every night. Digital and reality are ALWAYS different. Imagine the amount of grief Jackson could have avoided by not creating this ridiculous fantasy.

Here is a question that illustrates how you can push someone away via text and why you should NOT use texting to handle serious things.

Hi Mike,

I'll give you a brief history. Back during Christmas time, I asked a girl out (a casual friend who I've known for a few years). We had a great time (it was a very long date). She texted the next morning saying so. To my surprise, there was a ton of texting through the next few weeks. She would initiate a lot and we would go out a few more times afterwards. I especially used your tips from your book here. She would usually initiate the texting and sometimes we just talk about random things and the flirting was definitely there.

There was even a point where we would text multiple times a day and have daylong conversations. A few times she'd start off her day early in the morning with some random text to me.

About a month ago, we set up another date (through texting). She seemed a little withdrawn as she was busy at work (she went back to work after dinner). I didn't think anything was that unusual. We set up plans to go see an event for a week later and she said to "keep in touch." However, late that evening, she said she checked her schedule and wasn't able to make it. A few days later, I texted asking how her day was going and she replied very briefly. I sent a flirty text on Valentine's day with no response. Then just over a week later I sent a text asking how her weekend was going and there was no response.

Anyway that's a brief history, I'd appreciate your advice. I'm just a little unsure of why the texting has suddenly stopped and I kind of miss the random interaction. Should I just call or email / text her with something random again? Her birthday is coming up in a few weeks too. Let me know if there's anything extra you want to know.

Where does she live? Is she close to you?

I am pretty sure that there is another guy in the picture. The fact she didn't respond to your text on Valentines day is a huge sign that she was with someone else. The cooling you are experiencing from her is directly related to the fact that she feels as if she is cheating by staying in contact with you. This is silly of course and we need to convince her of this.

You did a great job with the texting before but unfortunately this is a situation that needs to be handled in person or... email if you must.

This is the problem with texting, it is awfully easy to ignore. Now, if multiple texts are ignored, a level of guilt starts to build and your target will want to avoid you. Therefore, EVERY text you send from this point on is making her feel upset and a bit sick towards you. So stop texting 100% and let her forget this feeling.

Now you need to figure out what is going on, why all of a sudden she went cold on you. I am putting my money on, another guy, but it could be a few things.

- Maybe your last date didn't go as well as you thought

- Maybe she lost her phone (doubt it)

- Maybe she is stressed out of her mind with something

- Maybe she just doesn't feel the same about you

The beginning of your relationship started with a lot of energy, lots of attention and tons of texting. A very fast start to any relationship will often lead to burn out, you have the control to slow things down and make her more interested by withholding more. Don't text back, don't call back, slow things down next time.

It strikes me that this girl is a bit young and very fickle, I imagine she changes her mind very quickly (hard to know without more detail from you but making my best guess), that can work in our favor when you contact again.

First: No contact for at least a week or two but if you have already done this we can move forward.

Next: We need to make contact in a way she cannot refuse. If it is appropriate show up at her work or "catch" her somewhere by "accident". So often situations like this have false tension built up, that can be broken just by a brief talk. This is best to do in person. All you have to do is be really friendly and extremely cool about everything, give her a hard time about not texting you back. Ask her directly, "You just disappeared on me! What, do you have a boyfriend now?" Now smile and laugh. Confront the situation directly so that she has to as well, 99% of the time it is something silly, that she overthought.

IF: You cannot run into her, you can contact her via facebook or email. I want you to be really nice and disarming, anything that puts up her defenses will result in her not responding. Let me know if you are going this route and I will help you do it.

So to reiterate, texting is not going to open this door, it will only close it further. You must make direct contact and lyse the boil of her hang up. As long as you are friendly and confident as hell, you can get her back on the hook.

Let me know what you decide to do.

-Mike

Getting them back on the line

Before we make a run for this, we need to remove what drove them away in the first place. You, showing too much need, and screwing up the balance. We need to mask our need, so first let's work on our poker face.

Step one - Put on your Poker face – Ever watch the TV show Poker After Dark? If you haven't, stay up sometime and observe the really freaky people dropping hundreds of thousands of dollars in Las Vegas poker tournaments. They are absolute masters of two things, reading the nuances in the behavior of other players, and disguising their own thoughts with misleading grunts, loaded comments, deceptive humor, or simply a lack of emotion hidden behind sunglasses and a cloud of cigar smoke.

Remember these guys are focused on two things, hiding their cards, and trying to guess what the other person is holding. Imagine if one of the players said, "I hate all these games, can't we just drop all the bullshit? Here are my cards, what do you guys have?" What would be the outcome? Would the game remain fun? Would the other players respond in kind? Would anything good come of this??

When you text too much emotion, show too much intention, or demand a certain outcome, you are essentially showing your cards. The game is no longer fun when one partner knows that you have a really weak hand and don't know how to bluff. You don't have to be as awesome as that other person, or NOT have the emotion, but you do have to hide your cards.

(Just like the woman earlier, a lot of people balk at this because they hate the idea of "the game". What they totally miss is that you simply do not have a choice. The game is constantly played whether you like it or not. Why? Because behind the deck of this game is your animal mind. You know, the one that is attracted to girls that treat you like shit. I can't really go into this too deeply since it is another book but trust me when I say that playing the game is necessary simply because you cannot think your way around or into attraction. Someone else is at the wheel, namely your animal subconscious mind)

80

Step two - Give it some time - Remember the major mistakes that people make texting? Like responding too soon, or too often, or not leaving the conversation first? These time-related mistakes scream that you are impatient, and emotionally less mature than the other person.

You know how you feel when that person isn't getting back to you? You know how suddenly their value goes up because they don't appear to care? Well it is time to reverse this, time to bring a little balance back in your court with a little patience.

Most of you just made a mild mistake and all you need do is give them a week. What this does is not only allow your last awful text, "I really like you and I don't understand why you are not texting me back??" to fade from memory, but shows that you have enough emotional control to chill for a bit.

(The reason why getting someone back only works 50% of the time is because people rarely change their original assessments of others. That is why if we can get the door open just a crack, we need to be a totally different person immediately)

Step three - Reestablishing safety - I think all of us understand why women are a bit fearful of the guy that comes on too strong. This guy appears to only be a few whiskeys away from date rape. Even if this isn't remotely true, women will avoid this guy just like you might avoid golfing in a lightning storm, sure it is a remote possibility but why risk it?

What most women don't understand is that aggressively pursuing and/or going emo, triggers a massive fear response in men as well. Seriously, you might be 100 pounds of tiny, but trust me he is afraid of you. Why? Because every man out of high school has had a woman go bat shit on him at least once, and if he even gets a whiff of this he is out!

Guys all know what I'm talking about, it's that girl that thinks anger will somehow force you into feeling the same way. Ha, ironically just 20 minutes ago a girl pulled this on me after wanting to see me last night and tonight, I said "no" two days in a row.

Her: Are you busy tonight?

81

Me: So sorry, today is a work day and I have so much to finish, is another night okay?

Her: You must have been tired from last night, what was her name? Anyway, hope you get a lot done.

Me: Hahaha... thanks for the guilt trip. Please don't text me if you can't control your emotions.

No guy wants to deal with a girl that is going to snap on him because he isn't responding to her script. If this girl wants to be back in my life she needs to prove to me that she isn't a nutter, but honestly because of the above text, it's too late.

Step four - Safety/funny – After your week of down time you can start to formulate ways to get your target back on the hook. The best way to do this is make light of the situation, NEVER again reference the offending text, be funny, and end in a question.

Remember the example I gave to Jackson?

So I haven't heard from you in about a week, and I got so depressed that I jumped off the roof to kill myself. Unfortunately, I live in a tent and it didn't work out to well. =) So how are things?

Above we make light of the situation by using lots of sarcasm and a little self-deprecation. It is a bit like an apology without having to bring up the offending past.

We don't reference the cause of the person's disappearance for the same reason we don't bring up how their dog died of testicular cancer. We don't want to illicit the feelings associated with your screw up. Don't bring it up, it never happened.

The funny part is glaze on the donut. We have removed the fear by making light of things, now we want to add a smile to their face and have it associated with us. Hopefully we will get a text back in the next 5 minutes.

Some examples for girls that you might enjoy:

Hey, haven't heard from you in a while! So I got a tattoo of your face on my left breast, want to see?? Hahaha (Just by making fun of being a psycho shows that you have enough introspection to not be)

So I planned this big elaborate meal to make you when I remembered, I can't cook! Shit... buy you a drink instead? (Guys love to have women buy them a drink because it happens so rarely, now once you got him there remember, A game!)

I told myself I shouldn't talk to you, but I keep having these sexual dreams about... =) (Great hook and although I tell women not to talk about sex, this is a last ditch effort, which might work since men are very much controlled by their sex drive)

Examples for guys:

So I met this guy that I thought would be perfect for you, he looks a lot like me but he always says the right thing. I think you should give him a shot. (Cute, apologizes nicely without referencing the past, would be good to use with an empathetic girl)

Hey I think I met your twin the other day, I asked her out but now she won't stop texting me! Got any advice? (Hahaha, that's funny. Good apology if you were the one texting her too often, nice setup to allow her to take a shot at you for texting too often, nothing like a little revenge to lead to forgiveness)

Crap! I must have been really drunk last night, I got your name tattooed on my back but I think I misspelled it. Gennifer isn't spelled with a G is it...? (Back to the ludicrous, if you can make fun of being nutty it is a great apology)

Safety/funny is not only good for getting someone back on the line but also excellent if you mess up. Cocky funny is not always the best especially if you are in the doghouse. They will not hear the funny, only the cocky, and it will backfire on you. The hook also is dangerous to use in this situation because they know your need and they might call your bluff.

There is one more option I would consider.

83

The Honest Approach

If you can word this right, it can be as effective as above. However, the best place to do this is from your FB or email account, not phone. Like I said before, keep your texting playful, not serious. The opportunity for misunderstanding of tone and meaning is just too great. At least with email you can be verbose enough to get the point across. With this said, if you do choose the email option you should go with something like this.

Hey, _____

I haven't heard from you in a while and I am guessing that maybe I made you feel uncomfortable? If that's the case I totally understand, I am not so skilled at communicating over text! =)

Just wanted you to know that I think you are great and it would be nice to keep talking. I will admit I like you, but if that isn't something you can return right now I understand. Just want you to know there is no pressure coming from my side, but it would be nice to have the chance to keep getting to know you more. Maybe we can have coffee or a drink sometime, my treat!

Hope this mail finds you well and I hope to hear from you soon.

-Mike

Obviously if this speaks to you more than trying to rekindle via text, go for it. Personally I think it is better to just start over, you blew it, learn from it and do better next time! But of course give it a shot and see what happens, and DON'T repeat this!

Got a question? Want to contact Mike?

Unfortunately, I can no longer answer questions for free. I get about five a day and I honestly don't have enough time to answer everyone. However...

I do phone consultations for 30-60+ min sessions at $1 a min. Just send me an email and we will schedule a time for you. =)

Look forward to hearing from you.

Mike Masters

mikethemasterdater@gmail.com

Made in the USA
Lexington, KY
22 July 2012